"Every parent affected by autism shou[ld read this book. It] answers the tough questions and gives eas[y-to-understand advice] that is honest and pertinent. A book like this is long overdue!"

— Hyndi Khomutetsky, MS, BCBA, Program Director

"This book not only addresses the aspects of growing into an adult that every child will face, it also provides a clear, behavioral, user-friendly approach on how to plan for your child's future. This book is geared to assist parents in setting their child up to achieve greater levels of independence and personal competence. Bobbi's step-by-step guide on how to plan for the inevitable should be required reading for anyone who has children with developmental delays."

— Nicole Geiger, MS, BCBA

"I am pleased to recommend this book to parents of older children with special needs. It is filled with helpful ideas, information, and strategies. The compassion and care the author has for these families is clearly evident in the thoughtful way the information is presented."

— Cherish Twigg, MS, BCBA, Managing Partner, Establishing Operations, Inc.

"A compass for parents/caregivers who feel lost or need redirection as they journey the road less traveled. Thank you for caring and sharing!"

— Mary Tracey, parent

"Having a child with autism, I have struggled picturing my son past his childhood. I've somewhat developed a mental block of him as an adult with this disability. Reading through Bobbi's book and completing the self-evaluating tasks have painted a much clearer picture. There does not have to be a fear for parents with kids on the spectrum. Bobbi made the worksheets simple and easy to complete. She is a true asset to her profession and our autistic community."

— Tiffany Watts, mother of ten-year-old son with autism

Autism,

ADOLESCENCE & ADULTHOOD

Finding the path to independence

Autism,

ADOLESCENCE & ADULTHOOD

Finding the path to independence

by Bobbi Barber, MS, BCBA

DEVELOPMENT SERVICES, INC.

Oviedo, Florida

Autism, Adolescence, and Adulthood: Finding the Path to Independence
By Bobbi Barber, MS, BCBA

Published by HigherLife Development Services, Inc.
400 Fontana Circle, Building 1, Suite 105
Oviedo, Florida 32765
(407) 563-4806
www.ahigherlife.com

ISBN 13: 978-1-935245-44-5
ISBN 10: 1-935245-44-9

Cover Design: Principle Creative

First Edition
11 12 13 14 — 9 8 7 6 5 4 3 2 1
Printed in the United States of America

I dedicate this book to all the families I have had the privilege of knowing and to their spectacular children, whom I adore and wish the happiest of futures.

Thank you

Dear Parents and Colleagues:

In writing this workbook I have spent my time and energy in engaging parents in the forward momentum of helping their children to become independent. There is an enormous amount of knowledge available about what works, what doesn't work, and what terminology should be used when discussing behavior and the behavior change process. Note that this workbook is not a book that focuses on terminology and the language used by behavior analysts. This book is dedicated to the parents and caregivers who attempt to engage proactively in their children's lives. Therefore, the language used is meant to assist you and not to be used as an applied behavior analysis (ABA) reference tool.

Parents and caregivers should also note that this workbook does not address the vital component of functional language or verbal behavior (VB). Verbal behavior is a lengthy, incremental process that requires the guidance of a trained behavior analyst. The tools and techniques used to promote functional communication are too comprehensive to address in this manual. If you have concerns or would like to add a communication element to your child's learning repertoire, please seek the guidance of a behavior analyst who specializes in verbal behavior. Their knowledge would be an excellent companion to this workbook.

Bobbi Barber, MS, BCBA

Acknowledgments

To Eric, my husband, thank you for all your love, support, and words of encouragement. You lift me up when I cannot lift myself. I love you.

To my son Caleb, you are my heart, my love, and my light. I love you.

A special thank you to all my friends and family who have helped me achieve my goals and discover my gifts. I appreciate all that you do and all that you are.

Table of Contents

Introduction

Welcome to the stage in life when the early intervention has passed and your little one becomes a child. For most people, looking back on the elementary, middle school, or high school years provides happy memories of "the best years of our lives." When we become parents, we look forward to creating those memories with our children. We dream of being in the stands at their big game, of watching them graduate, of taking pictures before the prom. Then the teen years actually hit, and parents are in a long struggle with their teenagers, who are learning to express their needs and cope with the mental, emotional, and physical changes going on in their lives. When you are parenting a teenager with special needs, these years take on a whole new set of challenges. This book was written with the intention of providing ideas for purposeful living and enriching activities specifically for families who have an adolescent or adult family member, loved one, or dependent who is affected by autism or a related developmental disability. My hope is that through the work you do in this book you will begin to experience the wonder and enjoyment this stage of life can bring you.

In parenting or teaching those with developmental disabilities, the primary focus is often on early education. By the time the teen years come along many families may feel left out or ignored. Unfortunately, for children past the age of three, many assessments, treatment programs, and facilities fail to provide the knowledge of where to continue in the education and treatment for growing children with a developmental disability who are behind in their learning. The development rate of social aptitude, educational goals, self-care, and independent functioning skills begins to slow as a child ages. The challenge for the caregiver lies in finding the motivation, dedication, and persistence in aiding children, teens, and adults in their journey to becoming self-sufficient. If you are experiencing any frustration about where to go, where to begin, or what to do, help is within your reach. If you have passed the three-year-old mark and your child is either a teenager or an adult, you can still take part in helping him or her shape a life that has independence and integrity.

Many books, seminars, and other sources of information for the parents of children with ASD (autism spectrum disorders) have the primary focus on early intervention, which takes place prior to three years of age. But what happens after your child exits early childhood and moves into the elementary school, teen, or early adulthood stage of life? Without much information or many ideas, families and caregivers can feel lost or angry, fearing that the person they love has been left behind. This workbook is for the parent, caregiver, therapist, or administrator who wants to give meaning, enrichment, and vitality to the life of an adolescent, teenager, or adult diagnosed with autism or a developmental disability.

The good news is that wherever your loved one is on the journey to self-sufficiency, progress can be made. You have all the power and ability to make a difference and every opportunity to make improvements and start creating independence. This book will help you to pick a starting point. Remember, learning takes place every day, all around us. The brain has an amazing ability to continue learning throughout the life span. For decades, it was assumed by many neuroscientists that adults' brains were hardwired, could not generate new cells, and could not significantly change. In the 1970s the science began to change in earnest, and we now know that the brain is not static but plastic. The brain is adaptable and capable of being reprogrammed.*

What neuroplasticity means for you and me is that we don't ever need to give up. There is no magic window of time that closes on a person's ability to learn. Certainly for all of us, including children with developmental disorders, it is easier to learn in the zero-to-four age range. But we can all be taught new tricks. Did you teach your grandmother to get online and send an e-mail? Have you had to adapt in your adult years to new technologies and new ways of doing things? Of course you have. Your adult or teenaged child can learn new techniques as well.

When I was just starting out in the field of developmental disabilities, my first job was working at a group home in an adult house for the severely developmentally disabled. In my time at that facility I experienced the stark reality that many of the individuals living in that home were completely unable to care for themselves. Their families could no longer care for them, not because they were physically or mentally incapable of learning the skills, but because either they were too aggressive or their families didn't have the resources or support to maintain the high level of care they required. Some clients were in their thirties and forties and lacked the ability to independently complete basic tasks like brushing teeth, bathing, getting food or drink, or even getting dressed without assistance. My job was to run these self-care and daily living skills for them everyday.

After that job I began working in the public school system with elementary students who were severely developmentally delayed, and I saw students at age nine who

* Meghan O'Rourke, "Train Your Brain: The New Mania for Neuroplasticity," *Slate Magazine*, April 26, 2007.

also lacked the ability to care for themselves in the basic ways. From my experience with the adult community, I knew it would be highly valuable for these elementary age children to start the process of independence so that they would be more functional at home with their own families at that age and in the future. Recognizing the need for those skills, I made it a part of their educational program.

These experiences created in me a desire to give parents the tools they need to help their children now in preparation for the future. My focus is to help you help your child in order for that child to remain at home as a functioning participant in your family. I wish for all families to have the option for their children to stay with them as long as possible. The thought of any of the children I work with being placed in a group home because they are a burden is deeply upsetting. Group homes are wonderful facilities doing fantastic work, but I want all individuals, whether they live in a group home or with their family, to have their dignity and independence. Having a child remain in the home to which she or he is accustomed should be a choice a family can make rather than having no options but full-time care.

I feel it is my obligation to tell all my parents that they have the ultimate responsibility to take control of helping their child learn those basic life skills. In my decade of work in this field, I have been continually disappointed by the lack of family involvement in the process of teaching. I do not intend to judge families; most of them are worn out from providing the daily care for their child themselves and discouraged by the lack of information and support available to them. I hope to inspire families to step up to the challenge by giving them the tools to successfully create independence in their loved one. It isn't easy, but I have seen what happens to adults who are incapable of caring for themselves and the suffering that causes for a family.

I hope that this workbook will be a starting point for any parent or caregiver who is in the position to help or train a person with a developmental delay who they have ever felt has been left out or left behind. With these tools in hand you can meet the challenges of adolescence and adulthood and enjoy your child for who he or she is and what he or she contributes to the family unit.

Note: To avoid overuse of the somewhat awkward "he or she," "him or her" construction, I'll be replacing some of these with alternating use of "he" and "she" throughout the book.

Part 1
The Path to Purpose

"So much has been given to me, I have not time to
ponder over that which has been denied."

—Helen Keller

Chapter 1

Finding Purpose

*T*he idea of purposeful living can be a last thought for many caregivers. With all the day-to-day activities and appointments that take place in your life, purpose is almost entirely lost. Children, teens, and adults can be moved around from school to home to therapy and back home day in and day out without much thought given to the purpose of their activities. Every person who cares for a developmentally disabled person is acting in that person's best interest. Adding the idea of "What is this going to accomplish?" or "What sense does this make?" or even "How is this going to benefit him?" will bring purpose not only to the child you care for but also to your daily tasks. Imagine the change you would experience in teaching teeth-brushing or shoe-tying day after day if you felt connected to your purpose rather than to the tedium of the task — if you were able to re-engage with a bigger purpose: *what this task means to my child's dignity and what learning this task will give to me and the others in my family*. Connecting to a higher purpose will fuel your ability to keep going with the task at hand.

As your child ages, the importance of creating independence grows exponentially. A ten-year-old becomes eighteen quickly, and before you know it you have a grown adult who needs to be able to function and operate with the least amount of help. Dependency will create stress for the caregiver as the child gets older, bigger, and stronger. The requirements of teaching new skills compound on an already overstressed person. By starting today and deciding you are going to make an effort to help your child, teen, or adult to be less dependent on you, you can be assured that she will be a part of your family for as long as possible.

Making sense of the never-ending cycle of home, school, therapy, sleeping, and eating, and starting over tomorrow, working toward unified, intentional goals, will help ease the stress of dependency you may be feeling. The intention here is never to judge or create more burdens but rather to get any parent or caregiver on track with a sense of purpose. Purpose will give meaning to the life of your loved one and to your daily life.

Living with dignity is a phrase we all know and have heard, but what does it mean? Look at your child and determine how capable he is of caring for himself. Ask yourself about your child's unique needs and abilities. When does it become undignified for children to wear pull-ups? How long should you have to wash their bodies, their hair, and tend to their personal hygiene before their sense of dignity has expired? The greater the level of disability, the greater the need to begin as soon as possible teaching the life skills needed to operate, function, and contribute to their own care and move toward independence.

The end goal is to help your child, teen, or adult become as independent as possible, not only performing life skills but also infusing those skills with the dignity and purpose each of us desires. Your own daily tasks, like grocery shopping, answering e-mails, attending meetings, doing lawn work, creating reports, and doing dishes, would be tedious (and often are) unless you can connect those tasks to a greater sense of purpose in your life. You do dishes because you value beauty and order in your home. You answer e-mails because you value doing your job well and creating good communication. It is the same for a teenager on the autism spectrum—brushing her hair herself is a trying task for someone with low muscle tone and ultra sensitivity in her scalp. Yet performing the task of brushing your hair has value when linked with the dignity of taking care of yourself and the purpose of presenting yourself to others in the community to form relationships.

Family Snapshots

In the Family Snapshots sections of this book you will see fictional pictures of families coping with some of the issues you may have. Here we can get a clear picture of what works and what solutions are available for the things that don't work. Below, the two very different families provide us a snapshot for creating purpose. One family has an over-scheduled life with many moving parts, and the other has a more developmentally disabled child who is more of a dependent, lacking a lot of necessary independence.

Family Snapshot

Meet the Baileys. They are a family of five: Mom, Dad, and their three children, Johnny, age ten, Abbie, age eight, and Nickolas, age five. Their average week is filled with a barrage of to-do lists and the hectic chaos of getting it all done: homework, appointments, laundry, dinner, chores, bathing, playing, cleaning, school, work, social engagements, birthday parties, holidays, and time spent with each other. This family also has the added stress of a developmental disability. One of the children needs a little more help than the others. There are more appointments to make, especially in the case of therapy sessions. It takes longer to get dressed, longer to eat dinner, longer to get out of the house, and more time is spent planning activities or making accommodations for doing things with the entire family.

The result of the Baileys' lifestyle is stress. They stress over lack of time, lack of energy, and a general lack of "enough." They sense that the problem lies in how they handle the one child who may need a little more—she either gets too much of the attention or not enough at all.

Abbie, the middle child, is the one with the developmental disability. She is nonverbal, not fully potty trained, doesn't play appropriately with toys or occupy herself with an individual activity for longer than twenty minutes. Needless to say, the family structure revolves around Abbie's needs and schedule. Mom is always hectically juggling the needs of the other two children while keeping Abbie occupied, but she worries that she is not doing everything right. She is concerned that she is not making Abbie's life one that is independent or self-sufficient and that she is losing valuable time. She fears that Abbie will never be able to care for herself and that ultimately she will have to take care of her well into Abbie's adult years. Mom also has the burden of wondering how Abbie's diagnosis is affecting John and Nick. They have to accommodate a lot for Abbie. Mom is aware that their needs often come second to Abbie's but doesn't know what else to do.

The Baileys are just one snapshot of a family living with a child who has a developmental disability. The diagnosis becomes the identity of the entire family. But what else is there to do? How can it not become the center of the entire family's life? It's hard to imagine another way of doing things. The helpless feeling associated with a family member who struggles to keep up with the pace of the rest adds to the strain of daily life. The solution lies in organization and family time management. Restructuring the family parts to work as one unit, despite a disability, will make significant improvements in the quality of life.

Solutions:

Consulting the Baileys, I would suggest organizing the daily life of all participants, keeping a journal or creating a poster that outlines their family's daily activities. Who is doing what at what time and where? Once they analyze where everyone is and what they are doing, the Baileys can create a visual aid that will help them truly see what is going on in their lives. Organizing takes time and effort, but the end result will help you gain control over the places you see need to be adjusted or changed.

The second step for the Baileys would be to *edit, edit, edit*! What is really necessary? I would not recommend cutting out specific therapies, but I would ask Mom and Dad to evaluate the purpose of each activity. Does horseback riding/occupational therapy/music therapy/floor time/ABA add any value to their child's life? What is she learning in the sessions? What are Mom and Dad learning? What are family members learning that is adding value to the overall family? How is that activity going to create independence or a greater sense of dignity for their child? If the Baileys cannot answer these questions, they would want to take the time to review each activity. If Mom and Dad, as the caretakers, or the siblings plainly need a break, then that may be something that is valuable to their sanity and therefore ultimately valuable to the entire family unit.

The point of editing is to simplify the day and take control. How can parents provide purpose to their child's life if they aren't positive of the purpose of the activities they place their child in? Editing is the caregivers' opportunity to find the areas that they can utilize in their big objective: providing meaning, purpose, and enrichment. If parents are bogged down by rushing around, they will not be able to take notice of where the opportunities lie to create independence. The family can and should spend the time to figure out what they want to participate in and what they do not need in their schedule. Avoid getting caught up in the routine and begin to gain control of what you are doing. Pay attention to your intentions or simply get in touch and remind yourself of your intentions. It is very easy to lose touch, but it is possible to connect with your life and remain present, active, and in touch with your family and purposes.

In the Baileys' case, if Abbie loves horseback riding, Mom can use the weekly horse therapy as an opportunity to imagine ways in which Abbie could eventually work in a stable. What are Abbie's strengths in this area of her life? Could she learn to make a vocation out of this hobby? Would that contribute to her long-term care?

Mom and Dad should also look more closely at all of Abbie's therapies. Is Abbie learning the skills needed to foster greater independence? Is she working on handwriting and tracing her name at eight years old? Could she be learning how to use zippers and buttons so that she can dress and undress herself? Have both parents come to an agreement or understanding of their wishes for Abbie? Have they both taken the time to have a conversation about the goals they are moving toward? If not, then those goals may never be reached. I encourage both parents or all caregivers involved to take the time and discuss your child or children and develop a plan that is most suitable for you both. This will definitely help the family to become unified and reduce the amount of stress placed on one person.

What about in your case? How are you taking an active approach in your child's therapy? Now is the time to analyze the short- and long-term objectives of the activities your children are involved in. If you really feel the therapies and activities you go to week after week have value, then use that value to the advantage of your child's future. You do not have to blindly accept the skills being taught. Ask yourself: How is he benefiting from this? What skills are going to emerge from this activity? What other, greater advantage can I make of this activity? Is there a future job or occupation that this activity could build into? How can I make the most of the time I am spending on this activity to create a more independent child?

My goal is for you to get to the center of your life's purpose. Why are you driving yourself crazy trying to get it all done? Is it realistic to try all these activities? Are they contributing to the overall goals needed for your child with special needs and the family as a whole? Ask yourself this: "What is this (fill in the activity) teaching my child? How does it improve her life right now and her life in the future?" You might find that the activities are vital and worth the pressure for a set amount of time, but then you will be in charge of the chaos. *We are choosing this activity for this period for achieving this specific goal. Once the goal is met, we will edit.* If you cannot come up with a logical reason for the activity, then maybe it needs to be edited out of your schedule now. Once you have edited your weekly or daily schedule down to the nitty-gritty essentials, organize the effort it requires to get it all done. From this point, planning is essential.

Family Snapshot

Meet the Carters. They are a family of three: Mom, Dad, and Tommy. Tommy is fourteen years old and his parents are in their forties. Tommy goes to a special needs school all day from Monday through Friday. At night, Tommy is completely dependent on Mom and Dad to take care of his needs. They prepare all his meals, wash, fold, and put away his laundry, clean up after him, bathe him, and take care of most of his other daily and self-care needs. Tommy has no "real"'

> *responsibilities around the home or for himself. Once he is home from school or activities, Mom and Dad let him have free rein over whatever he wants to do to fill his time. They have done this since Tommy was little.*

The grim reality of the Carters' situation is that Mom and Dad may not be able to maintain such a high level of care for Tommy indefinitely. Tommy is only fourteen, but soon he will be twenty-four, then thirty-four, and Mom and Dad will be in their fifties and sixties. What will happen to Tommy when they can no longer care for every detail? He will either enter a group home or assisted living facility, or maybe a family member will help. But is that really fair for Tommy or for the others who will have to care for all of Tommy's needs? Shouldn't Tommy, no matter his level of disability, have some responsibility over and participation in his own care?

For Tommy to live with dignity and purpose, he should have some independence in his own care. Since he is fourteen, there has been a long time when no demands have been placed upon him. This family may have a more difficult time getting Tommy to adjust to taking on his own self-care, but there are opportunities for this family to operate functionally. If the Carters can keep in mind the goal, which is to assist Tommy in becoming the most independent person possible, then they can look forward to a long life with Tommy being home with them for as long as possible.

The Carters will want to first take inventory of the skills Tommy possesses, build on those existing skills, and then plan out what and when to teach the remaining skills he needs to be in their home, functioning at an appropriate level.

Planning is the essential portion of organization. It's the structure and backbone of your life. If you plan for today and for tomorrow, then it all can fall into place. You will be prepared and have the ability to work your schedule and that of your children. But more importantly, your family will have the framework for their functioning as well. I know this is easier said than done, but good scheduling will serve you in answering the ultimate question: Do I want my child with a disability to be dependent or independent?

It is very important, even crucial, that you "get real" with your life situation. This includes being brutally honest with yourself about the situation at hand. In all my years as a behavior analyst and professional administrator, I have seen countless examples of parents who are in denial. They are in denial about their child's delay, about the future that inevitably lies ahead, about the amount of work it takes to accomplish their goals, and most importantly, about *their* ability to really take action. Even though this can sound a little harsh, it is true. Keep in mind that this harsh truth is the same light you would shine on your own life if things were not working for you. You would analyze your goals, evaluate your plans, and rework your tasks until you could meet your own goals.

The future will always come. There is no way to alter time or stop the clock. You are aging at the exact same rate as your child. If they aren't expected to learn the skills needed to function as close to independently as possible, then eventually you will lose the ability to care for them, and then group home or assisted living will shortly follow. If at ten years old your child cannot use the bathroom independently, then it is quite likely that he will not be going to drive a car in the next six years. By twenty, if your son or daughter is still dependent on you to complete the basic tasks such as getting up in the morning, getting dressed, or making breakfast, how can you expect that your child will ever be independent? A group home or a long-term-care facility may be next on your list of things to look at for the future.

Prepare to do the work. If you cannot commit to actually doing the work, then there is no point in starting, so be realistic about what you want to undertake, and have your vision of success clearly in mind. You can begin to work with your child at any age in order to give them the tools they need. It may be that their disability will still require individualized care. No matter what your child's ability or disability, your goal can always be to bring your child to their highest level of self-care possible.

Do you see the situation of the Carters or the Baileys in your own life, in yourself, in your children? Have you fallen hostage to the over-scheduling list, or are you on the other end, expecting too little of your child? It's possible to be both or to be neither or even to flip-flop between the two as life changes. Wherever you are right now, be confident in yourself. You *can* do it. With the right support plan in place you can be effective. So let's start planning. In the next chapter I'm going to ask that you complete two assessments. The first one is to learn more about yourself, and the second one will help you evaluate your child. Let the work begin!

Chapter 2

Discovering Who We Are and What We Are Capable Of

T he first tool I want you to work through is the Daily Schedule Evaluation. This is the tool I would have used with the Baileys. You need to analyze your life and the needs of your entire family before you can edit and shape a schedule that suits you, your child with a disability, and any other children you may have.

Worksheet 1: Daily Schedule Evaluation

I. Describe your typical day:

   Go to www.autismindependence.com to print out a journal log sheet or use a separate sheet of paper to log answers and/or task responses.

II. Break it down:

1. Easiest part of your day? Why?

2. Most difficult parts of your day? Why?

3. Part of the day that is the least structured/organized? Is this the easiest part of your day or the most difficult?

4. Part of the day that is most structured/organized? Is this the easiest part of your day or the most difficult?

5. Who are your helpers?

6. If you have help, in what ways do they contribute? How are they most helpful to you?

7. If you do not have help, do you think you need help?

8. If you do need help, where/how can you obtain it?

9. List the things you do for yourself. Examples: manicures, pedicures, exercise, shopping, etc.

10. How much time per day do you allow for yourself?

11. How can you make more time for yourself?

12. How valuable is it to you to have that personal time?

13. Discuss your frustrations. What is breaking you down or preventing you from moving forward?

14. Are there any physical issues that you struggle with?

15. Are there any mental/economic/social/family issues that you struggle with that hinder you from being effective?

16. What are the opportunities you have to participate in your child's therapy?

17. Are there any skills you could be learning alongside your child during therapy?

18. What are the things that get in your way? How do you become immobilized and in which situation(s)?

19. Are you able to release your stress, anxiety, guilt, frustrations? If so, who with?

20. Do you succumb to the pressures of other people's expectations?

21. How can you break those barriers if needed?

My Child Today

This second worksheet is the tool I would ask the Carters to use to assess the strengths and weaknesses of Tommy's skills today. Many parents know their children, but I want to encourage you to explore that knowledge and get to know them on a deeper level. I truly feel this will help you get in touch with all the positives and reassess the things you want to change. Remember, this will help you organize and tune in to the moment. I would also encourage you to have all the most important people in your child's life fill this out too. They may bring to light things you weren't in touch with and can also present new areas for growth and opportunity. Then I would recommend that in six months or a year you return to this tool and reevaluate the growth of your child's skills. Where has Tommy grown? What areas still present a struggle? I hope you will be surprised and encouraged by your child's ability every time you use this evaluation.

Worksheet 2: My Child Today

Go to www.autismindependence.com to print out a journal log sheet or use a separate sheet of paper to log answers and/or task responses.

1. Current age of your child.

2. Your child is affected by _____. Example: autism, Down syndrome, etc.

3. How has this diagnosis affected your child?

4. What are the great things about your child? List all the positive personality characteristics and traits that you admire and adore about your child.

5. What are your child's greatest struggles? List in order of the greatest struggles to the least.

6. What parts of the day are the hardest for your child?

7. What parts of the day are the easiest?

8. Are there any environments in which your child has the most difficulty? Why?

9. Are there any environments in which your child has the easiest time? Why?

10. How many persons interact/are a part of your child's treatment process? (Number of therapists/aides/persons helping with goals)

11. What are your greatest wishes for your child?

12. What do you want your child to accomplish in the next year?

13. What skill(s) do you think your child can/should learn that will make the greatest improvement in her life? (example: toileting, learning to play, etc.)

14. What skills does your child already have that you could help him improve on?

15. Where do you see your child five years from now? Ten years? Fifteen years? Twenty years?

16. Do you have a long-term plan for your child's care when she is an adult?

17. Where can your child work? Or what is your occupational hope for him?

18. Have you assigned/designated a caregiver for your child?

19. How long will you be able to care for your child/meet her day-to-day needs?

20. Do you have a designated caregiver, will, and estate plan should you no longer be able to care for your child?

After you have finished these worksheets, go back and study them. Where are there opportunities for you to make improvements? What areas need to be changed? This is your opportunity to get in touch with your life and to take a snapshot of your child. By doing this, you create a starting point for the change *you* want to see in your life and in your child's life.

Another important tool I recommend is keeping a journal. Journaling is a great way for you to keep track of what is happening in your life. Use it as a tool to vent, let loose, and express your deepest struggles, personal thoughts, and greatest achievements.

As you evaluate your lives, remember—*purpose*. That is the key word for you throughout this book. Figure out what is purposeful for your child and for your family, and then describe the steps it takes to achieve that purpose.

The next chapter will guide you through the concept of behavior. Yes, it is a concept! At least for a behavior analyst it is, so you need that insight to understand and manage behavior. As you learn how I and other behavior analysts think, your understanding of what you are doing and why you are doing it will also increase. When you reconnect with your purpose behind behavior modification, you will be empowered to keep up the good work.

—————————— *Part 2* ——————————

The Path to Planning

———————————————————————

"*People take different roads seeking fulfillment and happiness. Just because they're not on your road doesn't mean they've gotten lost.*"

—Dalai Lama

"*The most common way people give up their power is by thinking they don't have any.*"

—Alice Walker

Chapter 3

Behavior What?

*I*n my experience as a behavior analyst I have encountered many parents who desire to work with their child but who are hindered by issues of disruptive behavior. Many children have or will display behaviors that interfere with forward progress and cooperative functioning within the family environment. Parents can feel confused, overwhelmed, or defeated by many of these situations. This may be due to the sudden onset of the behavior, the inconsistency with which the behavior occurs, the level of harm or danger the behavior poses, and even whether they are irritated by the disruptive behavior.

I feel it is important to acknowledge the view of the parent because I understand the way you view your child. As a parent you hold a lot of emotions, experiences, victories, and love for your child. You may even have feelings of guilt, anxiety, or frustration from the years of struggle or difficulty that come with having a child with developmental disabilities. You could also experience feelings of contentment and joy in what you have already worked on and be ready to take the next step. And you probably feel a combination of all these emotions when you look through the lens of a parent at your child's life. Many parents secretly feel guilty or ashamed of those feelings from the overwhelming nature of having a child with developmental disabilities. You are not alone. It is okay to have several reactions to the things your child does or doesn't do. It can be a challenge to get up every day and face the world when you feel time is against you. You may feel like you are swimming against the current. Remember that over time, we all lose our determination and can become tired of the fight. I meet parents who feel guilty because their child is doing great with his behavior training as well as parents who struggle with anxiety about their child's seeming lack of improvement. If you are that parent who hides in the closet with dark feelings of sadness and grief for the life you have been given, take comfort, because you are not alone. There are a lot of families who carry around the emotions you experience.

You should hear that it is not wrong to feel the variety of emotions. What is awful is letting it get the best of you and prevent you from moving forward. Staying static in time and not doing the best you can to prepare for the days ahead will only compound your future anxiety, stress, and anger. Dealing with the difficulties of an adolescent child is not easy but neither is the burden of a full-grown adult who is still completely dependent on you to care for his every need. Give yourself permission and room to feel your emotions. There are also moments to act, and taking positive action will be a way to move through the difficult emotions and see results.

Over the years I have encountered many families who have yet to consider their future and the future of their child. They are innocently holding on to the notion that their child is only a child and will never be more, and as a result they make excuses for why their child cannot learn how to care for herself. The focus becomes on keeping the child happy in the moment and not ever pushing him to do more. We are seeing this more and more in typical children as well—both parents are working and exhausted, and an evening is spent with take-out food and kids playing video games until bed rather than dinner together, homework, and playtime. I completely understand that parents are doing things out of love, but what constitutes "happy" changes over time and is completely subjective. What is happy? Is happy spending hours self-stimming, watching movies without limits, or having access to anything they desire without ever hearing the word "no"? By not placing demands on a child or requiring her to participate in her own independence, you are essentially setting up a life for that child as a long-term dependent. Never having independence means never experiencing dignity. I don't know any parent who would wish their loved one to experience complete helplessness.

I encourage you to resist the urge to create excuses for inabilities. Having a disability does not equal lack of capability. The only good excuses are medical ones, such as when a child has a seizure disorder or another medical situation that excludes him from participation in some activities. I will bet you there are options available to a child in such a case. For example, being on a special diet doesn't mean a twelve-year-old boy cannot learn to prepare a meal or snack for himself. It just means the items he can choose from need to be preselected. In addition to that, he can also clean up after he has prepared the meal, clean up after the meal has been eaten, learn to wash dishes, load the dishwasher, wipe down counters, and even take out the trash.

When you treat your child with autism as you would any person living in your life and home, you are telling her that you value her contribution. When you expect her to participate in the chores and activities to care for herself to her best ability, you create dignity for your child. Having high expectations creates high hopes and is an excellent expression of your love for anyone in your care.

Being a behavior analyst allows me to see things from a nonemotional standpoint. I have learned the tools needed to analyze behavior. To do that, I consider the behavior itself, along with the environment prior to and immediately following the behavior, separate from the child. The child and the child's behavior are two different things. By understanding this, you can remove the assumptions of character that you place on your child in the moment a difficult behavior is occurring. From that I develop interventions to either increase behavior deficits (behaviors I want to occur more frequently) or to decrease behavior excesses (behaviors I would like to occur less often).

Take a moment to go deeper than bad behavior or unwanted behaviors and begin to look at everything as a behavior unto itself: breathing, yelling, running, clapping, hitting, standing. Every action that is observable and measureable is behavior. If I can see you do it and measure it by counting the number of times a behavior occurs or the length of time a behavior occurs, then it is indeed a behavior.

It is very important for you to understand how a behavior analyst views behavior and the behavior change process, because it will help you in invaluable ways as a parent or caregiver. Taking the time to learn these tools and practicing how to become more observant in your efforts to create independence will pay off.

As I said earlier, the behavior itself, the environment before the behavior, and the environment immediately after are the most influential in the behavior change process. Remember, behaviors are things we all do; this includes all the things your child does too much of, too little of, or not at all.

The starting point for you to effect change in behavior comes when you take a look at the critical element present with every behavior: the environment. The environment is *all* the things present during the behavior of interest. This can include anything: the people, the objects, the temperature, the lighting, the noise, the conversations, and even the paint on the walls. Have you ever thought, "My daughter only behaves a certain way in certain places"? For example, "Every time we go to the grocery store, Stacy screams and runs away. She never does this at home." If you can observe this unemotionally, then you can essentially pinpoint the element of the environment that contributes to the behavior. This will be your greatest advantage in the effort to make improvements. You will develop the skills you need to understand your child, the behavior that is taking place, and ultimately the tools needed to change the situation for the better. So remember, the environment has the ultimate influence over behaviors exhibited. Divide the situation or any situation into two pieces: the environment before the behavior and the environment immediately following the behavior. The environment before the behavior, or the setting event, is important to take notice of because in some cases it can help you predict the behavior. Ask yourself, "What is taking place before? What elements are present? What items are present? Sounds? Smells? People?" All these items plus others can and may contribute to your child's and your own behaviors. Let's look a little closer at the environment and the effect it has on behaviors.

Environment example: the shower. What behaviors occur in the shower? Hair washing, washing your body, shaving, turning on the water, picking up the soap, turning the shampoo bottle upside down to get the shampoo out. A lot of things occur in the shower, correct? You do not wash your hair in the backyard or at the grocery store. I know that sounds silly, but it demonstrates the environmental context in which certain behaviors occur. School is the setting event for dozens of certain behaviors that do not occur at home or in the car. Your home is also a setting event that can change from room to room. The bedroom sets up your behaviors in a way that is not the same as the kitchen or the bathroom.

This is also true for times of day. We all behave differently at different times of day. The alarm going off in the morning signals many behaviors—getting up, brushing teeth, making coffee, and getting dressed. For many people, those behaviors don't happen at six in the evening. Different events happen at different points in time, and timing can become a tool for your success. It is a good idea to practice the things you want to teach your child as close as possible to when the event would naturally occur. For example, establishing a solid going-to-bed regimen would mean that a series of events occurs at a particular time of day. Showering or washing up, getting jammies on, brushing teeth, cleaning up toys, setting out clothes for the next day, or nightly chores could be included in this time of day. Pick skills to teach, organize yourself, and then stick with it. If you practice picking up clothes off the floor on a random day whenever the time allows, that will not teach your child what is clearly expected of him. If you choose this as a skill to teach, pick the time of day you want that skill to be used, in the environment you want it to occur, and stick with it. If you find yourself using excuses like you are too tired or your other children have homework, then don't do it. Don't waste your time setting goals that you cannot teach. This is just wisdom, not judgment. You have many different skills to teach and a household to run and a job to do—set yourself up for success by choosing the skills you can teach. Then you need to amend your expectations. Don't expect the result to be different: The toys or clothes will still be there for you to pick up later. Remind yourself that you've decided you are going to teach that skill later, and don't frustrate yourself by wishing it was done already. Give yourself reasonable goals and the expectations to go along with them.

If you want to teach the skill of picking up but you have a lot of other things on your plate, simplify the task. Start with picking up only a couple of items, limiting the area to be cleaned to a small area, or choosing a different part of the day. If your problem lies in behavior outbursts or negative responses, we will get to that later. But remember the rules still apply: If you choose to address it, stick to it!

One of the tools in the previous section asked you to list the times of day when your child has the most difficulty and the times when he has the least difficulty with his behavior. Think about those times and try to envision the environment surrounding each time. Is your child at home? At school? Who is present in that environment? What is taking place?

Family Snapshot

Jessica has the most difficult time around 4 p.m. She sits in the car with her mom and older sister Monday through Friday as she rides home from school. During the 30-minute car ride she engages in crying and rocking behaviors. Most of the time she has her fingers to her ears and sometimes bangs her head on the window. The other daughter, Carrie, whines and complains about Jessica. Carrie wants to talk to her mom without Jessica crying or rocking. When Jessica cries or head bangs, Mom becomes very frustrated and irritated. This time of day is one that Mom dreads and that causes her much stress. She wants to talk to Jessica about her day and create an opportunity to have family time with her two daughters. Mom would really like it if they could interact positively. To her that looks like riding together, talking about their day, singing along with the radio, and having her girls engaging with each other.

From Mom's perspective this time of day is stressful. The car ride home seems to never end. If Mom can learn to look at the situation with her new tools of analyzing the environment, she can begin to modify the situation and understand it without adding to it the emotions of stress, anger, anxiety, or even sadness for having those daily feelings.

Let's look at this scenario with our behavior analyst's lens. The first thing to realize is that there are three people whom we can look at from a behavioral perspective. Mom is engaging in her own behaviors; the same goes for both Jessica and Carrie.

25

They are all sharing the same environment and having different behaviors due to that environment. Your behaviors are a part of the environment that will have an effect on the behavior of those around you. The environment is a constantly moving, interactive entity. You have an effect on it as much as your child. So don't forget to look at your own behavior as much as you look at everyone else's behavior.

Mom's Environment The CAR	Mom's Behaviors	Jessica's Environment	Jessica's Behaviors	Carrie's Environment	Carrie's Behaviors
Radio on	Singing along	Radio on	Fingers in ears	Radio on	Singing along
Windows up		Windows up	Head banging	Windows up	
Seat belts on		Seat belts on		Seat belts on	
A/C set to 76		A/C set to 76		A/C set to 76	
Family pet there (lap dog)		Family pet there (lap dog)		Family pet there (lap dog)	
Backpacks shoved in at feet		Backpacks shoved in at feet		Backpacks shoved in at feet	

In the above example all three of them are in the same environment and they are all having reactions to that environment. Jessica is banging her head on the window, Mom is asking her to stop, the radio is on so that Carrie can sing along with the music, the dog is barking at the other cars going by, Mom is fidgeting to adjust the air, the windows, the radio, the school bags, trying to figure out, while in a stressed state, how to improve the conditions of that environment so that all persons present are functioning in a way that is calm and cooperative.

So what is cooperative to Mom? She would like for Jessica to sit up straight without screaming or hitting her head on the window. She wants the dog to sit calmly on her lap, and she wants to hear about Carrie's day without her complaining about Jessica. Basically she wants what we all want: peace, cooperation, and cohesion in this particular part of the day. This is motivating to Mom because it makes her less stressful. When she isn't feeling stressed, she looks forward to being with her girls.

To make improvements in the afternoon pick-up routine, I would suggest to Mom that she start by making one change at a time so that she can identify the environmental trigger for Jessica. I would choose Jessica first because her head banging behavior needs to be addressed as the priority.

Day One: Leave the dog at home. Note Jessica's reaction, your reaction, and Carrie's reaction. The barking could be a trigger for Jessica.

Day Two: Turn the radio down or even off. Note the responses.

Day Three: Have an all-quiet car ride home, a good opportunity for Mom to enjoy the silence. Set it up for Carrie to have a special car ride home with a coloring book or other activity. Then reinforce Carrie's sacrifice in the car when she gets home with one-on-one time with Mom in her room.

Day Four: Provide Jessica with headphones or a special item that she's attached to.

Day Five: Bring a snack. Hunger could be a trigger for Jessica.

Day Six: Keep the car warmer.

In the above example of analyzing the environment, Mom paid close attention to the car environment and isolated the elements as well as possible. Along the way she may have found out the things that were triggers for Jessica.

When you discover what triggers the behavior, you will have a range of options for how to help your child cope in an environment. We will look at solutions in the following chapter's worksheets; just know that your trigger hunt is another key to your success.

New environments can create a variety of reactions reflected in your child's behaviors. Reactions may vary widely from place to place, time to time, or even without any predictable pattern. You may have trouble identifying what the specific trigger is, but there is always one present. You may have also found yourself saying, "Jimmy always acts out with his sister but not with me and his father." This is an example of how people in the environment can also have an effect on a child's behavior. An environment is made up of more than place. People, colors, sounds, smells, and times of day are all a part of the environment.

You may not always be able to anticipate or avoid environmental triggers. However, being aware of them will help you get out of the cycle of blaming emotions, feelings, or unrelated events on the behavior of concern. Yes, your child may appear to be unhappy to you, but assigning feelings rather than concrete static observable information will not help you redirect, avoid, or correct the situation.

Family Snapshot

Tommy's mom has said: "Tommy would be sad if I didn't take him to McDonald's every afternoon for French fries. I always go, because I don't want him to be unhappy." Tommy cries, screams, and rocks violently when he is denied French fries. Therefore, each day Mom or Dad goes the same route home and stops at the same McDonald's to get the same order of fries. It is now a ritual. When Mom and Dad assign emotions to this situation, they essentially remove themselves from the situation. This is an emotional situation, so there's nothing I can do about it. The issue of emotion can have relevance, but to change the behavior they will have to realize that the environment and all the people and items in it are what ultimately motivate Tommy's behaviors, and not his emotions. When Tommy is denied something he wants, he begins to engage in the behaviors that have previously resulted in him getting what he wants. His behaviors serve the function of getting to the items he wants. Tommy has used his ability to communicate (crying, screaming, and rocking) to get exactly what he wants in the moment from the people who can provide those items, and Mom and Dad are reinforcing those avenues of communication.

The most difficult part of being a parent can be in the separation of emotion from situation. It is a trap for parents to think they are always at fault or that they are the reason behind the difficult behaviors. Learning to evaluate the environment and make modifications to improve the situation is a skill that all our children use effectively to get what they want. Analyzing the environment and changing it is a skill you can learn to use to benefit your child and yourself.

In the application of behavior therapy, we exclude feelings, not because therapists are cold and heartless beings, but rather because we need to be objective and therefore productive. By saying that Tommy screams because he is sad is not helpful in figuring out an environmental influence at the time the behavior is occurring. When we remove emotions, we provide a framework for thinking to parents and caregivers who are trying to make changes to improve the lives of the children they love and care for.

At this point, I hope you are forming a mental list of what you want to teach your child. This is the time to wonder about the skills and essentials that will transform your child into the independent, self-sufficient person you desire her to be. Identify a skill that would be pivotal in creating the most change in your child's life. This is going to be your starting point.

Family Snapshot

Sara is mommy to Steve. Steve is thirteen years old. He has limited communication, few self-care skills, and little ability to entertain himself. Currently, he can toilet himself, wash his hands, eat a meal while staying clean, and maneuver his way functionally in his home. He enjoys playing on the swing set in his backyard. He self-stims with strings and spins in circles constantly when left unengaged. Sara is most interested in having Steve learn to bathe himself, get dressed independently, and brush his teeth. She would like him to have appropriate play skills in the afternoon and on the weekends when she or her husband cannot directly engage him.

Steve has many positive attributes. I would suggest to Sara that the one skill that would give him the greatest sense of independence at his age and provide him with dignity would be to teach him to bathe himself without any help. He is thirteen years old, and it is time he learns to take care of his body without the help of another person. Not only will this help out Mom and Dad, but Steve will experience greater self-sufficiency that will give him confidence and skills that apply to other issues. Bathing skills will also extend from this point in his life and serve him throughout adulthood.

The next step would be for Sara to identify all the behaviors associated with independent bathing by breaking the skill down into all the smaller components. Every behavior needed to complete the task needs to be identified and evaluated for training/teaching. Be specific about all the skills it takes to wash independently.

It is crucial that you make this as detailed as needed depending on the functioning level of your child. If your child has the overall concept of showering and you want to ensure that the details are being completed, then you may have a looser format of goals. If your child needs the extra help of every step being explained, then you will start there. The program will be designed by you, and therefore it has to be realistic enough that you can and will follow through with it as well. Remember what we talked about earlier about being realistic? If you cannot dedicate the time it takes to teach this skill, then this is not the one to start with.

Here are two ways this skill could be taught:

1. The Simplified Task List:

   • Go to shower

   • Turn on water

   • Get in

   • Wash hair

   • Rinse hair

   • Wash body

   • Rinse body

   • Turn off water

   • Get out

   • Dry off

   • Get dressed

2. The Dense Task list:

   • Go to bathroom

   • Take off clothes (this can be broken down to each individual clothing item)

   • Turn on water (if you choose to use the denser schedule, I would suggest setting the water temperature for them prior to entering the shower/tub).

   • Step into the shower

   • Get wet

   • Pick up shampoo

   • Open the shampoo

   • Pour shampoo into hand

   • Continue the list…

This may be a tedious ordeal, but it is very important that you take the time to identify the skill you want your child to learn and then break it down in the ways in which they can be successful and teach to mastery. The way you communicate the list to your child will vary depending on how she best receives information. You can read the list to your child or post it in the bathroom. You could make a checklist on a dry erase board for him to check off or create visuals to go with the instructions. How your child learns best will be the best way for you to use this task list tool. If a child cannot bathe herself at ten years old or twenty-five years old, then she will never be independent. You can get your child to the point of independence. That independence is a great advantage not only to him but to you. It will make your life easier if a person you care for can care for himself.

As a behavior analyst I want to give parents the gift of our way of thinking. When you modify your thinking by temporarily removing your emotions to shift your thinking to analyzing, you not only give your emotions a rest, you come up with solutions. I would like for you to view behavior from an analytic point of view. This means looking at behavior void of emotion and guessing about its origins and what the behavior may mean. Johnny spins in circles because he loves to do it. Becky cries only when she is sad. In the behavior world, making assumptions leaves a lot of room for interpretation. By looking at behavior through a different set of eyes, you provide yourself with a new technique for defining the situation in which it occurs, understanding the motivation behind the behavior, and discovering the tools to modify the outcome.

Behavior is anything an organism does. Translated, that means everything we do is a behavior: blinking, sleeping, yelling, drawing, walking, laughing, playing, climbing, sitting, standing—everything that a living organism can do. Trying to remain emotionally neutral when defining behavior will help you when you find yourself in a "hot" situation filled with yelling or tantruming. It may not be easy to separate yourself emotionally from your child. It may be even more difficult in the midst of a difficult situation like a public temper tantrum. When you are uncomfortable in a situation, being calm and trying to observe the moment from a behavioral point of view will give you tools that help you cope. When you have grown accustomed to this skill, I promise it will help you, even enable you to make a significant improvement in the situations outcome.

Family Snapshot

In the grocery store Jamie decides she wants a toy and Mom really doesn't want to purchase the toy at this time. The resulting situation is a full-blown tantrum by Jamie, who cries, throws herself down in the aisle, and repeats over and over, "I want a toy."

> *Mom is embarrassed because people are looking at her. She wants to stop Jamie from yelling and she wants to hurry up and get out of the store. Her solution is to give in and hand Jamie the toy. When she does this Jamie stops crying and yelling, stands up, and is the image of the perfect child the rest of the trip.*

Now, from a behavior analyst point of view, I see this situation with an entirely different set of eyes. The tantrum served a purpose for Jamie, a way of accessing that toy. Mom just reinforced, or taught, Jamie exactly how to get it. I would suggest that Mom evaluate the situation. If she really didn't want to buy Jamie the toy, then she should have refrained from doing so. Now if it wasn't a big deal, then why waste all that time with the tantrum in the first place? If you know you are going to give in, do not wait to teach your child how to get what they want in a manner that is socially unacceptable to you. When parents give in, it does so much more harm than good. Consider before you enter the store, mall, or wherever you are going what the triggers are for your child. Are there items in this store my child is going to want? Decide what you are willing to do and what you are not willing to reinforce and then stick to it. Easier said than done, I know, but why waste time and energy? Tell your child what you expect and be prepared to back it up.

When you think about behavior, I want you to focus on two areas: the behaviors you want to happen less often and the behaviors you want to happen more often. Some behaviors to decrease can include yelling, hitting, playing video games, and running off. Behaviors you would like to see happen more often include getting dressed, doing laundry, making a bed, taking medications, playing with toys, and participating in community outings. Try to focus in on the activities that create independence for your loved one.

After you can observe the situation without emotion or assumptions, you can begin the process of understanding why those behaviors occur. This is the part where we figure out the functions of behavior. Remember, behavior doesn't just happen. There is always a function or purpose. From a behavioral perspective the function of all behaviors can be found in one of four things:

1. Attention

2. Access

3. Escape

4. Self-stimulation

Let's break that down into real-life examples.

1. Ways that behaviors function for *attention:* These may include talking, whining, crying, pulling, pushing, tantrumming. People talk to have the attention of others. Whining and crying are ways that children try to get our attention. Attention can be very reinforcing and valuable to all of us. Do you raise your hand to get attention during a meeting? Clear your throat to make yourself known in a room? These are ways of getting *attention*.

2. Ways that behaviors function for *access* (obtaining the items/activities of desire or need): Ways of getting the things they want or need can show up in your children by way of asking, shouting, climbing (as on the counter), tantrumming, screaming, crying, yelling, running away. Please note that the same behavior, such as yelling, can serve multiple functions. Someone can cry to get your attention, cry to get you to go away, and/or cry to get the toy they want.

3. Ways that behaviors function for *escape:* These may include ignoring, running away, walking away, screaming, tantrumming, hitting. Escape means getting away. Children will hit to leave a situation. They will ignore you until you go away or tantrum to get out of doing something. Does any of this sound familiar? Think of yourself and other adults you know and you will see *escape* as a function of behaviors. Do you have a tantrum when someone cuts you off in traffic? Do you walk away from a difficult conversation?

4. Ways that behaviors function for *self-stimulation:* These may include spinning, flapping, rocking, repetitive behaviors, watching TV, playing video games. *Self-stimulation,* or stimming, is repetitive behavior that is soothing or stimulating. These behaviors are not always detrimental. Yes, they may be embarrassing, but that doesn't mean they need to be eliminated. You can set parameters for when certain activities are allowed, but completely eliminating them may be impossible or even unethical. Again, apply this concept to yourself and other adults you know. Do you need to have the TV on and your feet up after a hard day? Do you need the radio playing while you work? You are soothing or stimulating yourself in order to function in an environment or situation.

Family Snapshot

Billy is ten years old. He has a developmental delay with limited communication skills. He often runs away from his parents in public situations, and at home he is constantly disrupting his parents and siblings. This is what the behaviors look like: elopement, running away from parents, darting away when they are not looking at him, pulling free of any hand holding or attempts to be held back. His home disruptions include loud yells until someone comes to find him and pulling or knocking items off tables, counters, walls, or desks. This occurs when he is both alone and when he is in the room with his family. The result of Billy's behaviors is a lack of interest by any family members in going to public places. Often arrangements are made so that Billy stays at home or in the car with one of the parents while the rest of the family goes shopping and does errands. At home, the environment has been voided of a lot of decorations. Billy's siblings lock their rooms so he can't get in, and areas of the house have been blocked off. Billy has limited access to situations in the outside community and within his own home.

Billy's parents have done this not to be mean but to preserve his and their sense of safety, security, and emotional well-being. These limits reduce the amount of stress in their lives.

How can this family be helped? What can be done to make improvements? From a behavior perspective I want to know the function of Billy's behaviors. The behaviors function as his way of communicating with the rest of the world. It's his way of saying "I want that," "I need your help," "I'm hungry." Because Billy may lack the vocal ability to say the mentioned things, he has figured out a new way to express himself. He runs, darts, and pulls away to go to the toy section, the food section, or whatever part of the store he wants to go to. At home he pulls down items and yells to gain attention from his family or to get an item from the refrigerator. When he successfully gets what he wants, he learns that this is an effective way to communicate. Billy has no idea that his family members are pulling their hair out from stress; he only knows that what he is doing is working for him.

I would not want to make emotional assumptions about why Billy does the things he does. I would avoid saying he yells because he's sad or lonely. Those emotional states do not attribute a function to his behavior. By stepping back and looking at Billy's behaviors from your new point of view, you can now say Billy runs away in stores because he goes to the toy section. Billy yells to access the attention of his siblings.

By looking at the situation for what it is in the moment, you can define the function of the behavior. Once you have identified the behavior targeted for increase or decrease and identified the function, then you are on your way to making significant improvements in the future occurrence of that behavior.

Family Snapshot

Seven-year-old Timmy is very cute, with a deceiving smile. He has big blue eyes that make you just want to give him everything. Let's also not forget the cheeks. They are beyond adorable and add to the feeling of maternal longing to do everything for him, give in to every want, and enable him to not do much for himself.

Timmy pulls on Mom's arms, legs, shirt, even her hair. He does this all day long, when Mom is on the phone, making dinner, getting dressed, in the car, at the store. Mom always responds to this. She gives him eye contact, a vocal response, and basically complies with any attempt Timmy uses in his little bag of tricks.

It's easy to figure out Timmy's function or motivation. Did you guess attention? It would appear that Timmy pulls and tugs on any part of Mom when he wants her attention. And what does he get? That's right folks, her attention. She provides him with the good stuff in her eye contact, her verbal responses, and even in her body language every time she attends to Timmy's request for it. Now, is there any harm in this? I'm not going to judge Mom for her continued response to Timmy, but I would pose this question to her: "What is Timmy being taught?" Essentially, Timmy is learning how to get attention. What he isn't learning is how to functionally communicate to a variety of people in a variety of situations that would be considered socially acceptable as his life goes by. When he's thirty, should he be pulling on people to get something? Probably not. I would suggest that we teach Timmy how to gain attention and how to get the things he wants appropriately.

A child on the autism spectrum is only employing extreme forms of the functions of behavior. The functions of behavior are normal and effective and something you use every day. The child in your care is using extreme forms to communicate because that is the tool available to her. When you give her more tools and reinforce those tools' effectiveness, those behaviors will change.

Use Worksheet 6: The Behavior Assessment, located in the appendix, if you are experiencing the desire to work on or evaluate behaviors targeted for decrease. It will help you narrow your focus and provide insight to the before and after.

Chapter 4

Skills and Starting Points

*N*ow that you understand the concepts and functions of behavior, you can successfully apply the skills that behavior analysts use to change behaviors. Yes, you can! Knowing where to start is the next challenge. Having an idea of what you want to accomplish can give you either insight or confusion. You know your child/teen/adult better than anyone, so the first step is to take inventory of what he already knows and can do well. The following sections are meant to help you figure it all out. This is your opportunity to go through each part of your child's repertoire and assess those behaviors, analyze them, and provide a guide for what needs to be taught.

Inventory

What can my child do without any assistance? My child picks up items around the house and places them in an appropriate spot, sorts laundry, gets up in the morning without help.

Is this activity performed repeatedly or occasionally? Every day my child performs these tasks.

How long did it take for my child to learn this skill? She is ten years old and we have been practicing these items pretty much daily for the last couple of years.

How many people can my child do this skill for? He has been able to perform this skill for me consistently and sometimes for others.

Are there any instances where my child will not/refuses to do this activity? She does these things only in our house. I have not seen her perform these actions in other environments.

Roadblocks/obstacles (such as failure to generalize learned skills to other people, places, or environments, special diets, any handicaps, etc.). Sometimes she gets distracted with other activities, such as stimming. She will stop and has to be reminded to finish the task. When other people are in our home, she will not do any of the tasks.

Worksheet 3: The Skills Inventory

Go to www.autismindependence.com to print out a journal log sheet or use a separate sheet of paper to log answers and/or task responses.

Inventory of Skills and Abilities

1. Age of child/teen/adult

2. Likes

3. Interesting activities

4. Barriers/obstacles

5. What can my child do without any assistance?

6. Is this activity performed repeatedly or occasionally?

7. How long will my child attend to a task without interruption?

8. How long did it take for him to learn this skill?

9. How many people can she do this skill for?

10. Are there any instances where he will not/refuses to do this activity?

11. How can this be turned into a functional activity or occupational goal?

12. How many smaller steps can this be broken down into?

13. How many opportunities will she have to practice this skill?

14. How many people will he have to perform this skill for?

15. What kind of special training do I/other participants need?

16. How am I going to do this?

17. Do I need help?

18. If so, who?

19. How much help?

20. What is my time line for this being accomplished?

Use this time to closely evaluate the current functioning level of your child. Do not focus yet on the future or even the past; you can only control what is in the now. What is your child capable of now? Use your child's history of learning when evaluating what to teach, but focus on today and set your goals toward the future.

Organization

You need to organize your plan for implementing behavior change. This can be difficult even for a person with the best intentions. Please do not overlook your ability to take control of your situation. If you need a kick in the butt, this is it—get organized! This doesn't mean getting a fancy day planner or a scrapbook. Keep it simple and use a method or organization tool that works for you. Develop a plan, break it down, and then work the plan. Be realistic about what you are willing to devote yourself to. If you cannot stop and take the time and effort to teach the skill, then failure is waiting for you. Set yourself up for success.

This portion of the manual is designed to help you decide what you want to teach your child. There are several assessment tools on the market that are more geared for younger children, so I think it would be helpful to have ideas that pertain to the adolescent, teen, or adult. Many skills can be taught that have transitional purpose in the areas of leisure, independent living, or even a vocation.

The following is a list of potential skill areas to teach your loved one so that he or she can be as independent as possible. There are a lot of skills listed, but don't become overwhelmed if your child cannot do all of them. Pick the ones that have the most meaning to your family and start there. Of course, feel free to add any that you do not see on the list and that you feel are important.

Check off what your child can do in order to decide what to program for.

Worksheet 4: The Skills and Starting Points

Go to www.autismindependence.com to print out a journal log sheet or use a separate sheet of paper to log answers and/or task responses.

Visual Abilities

Blank boxes are purposed for parent fill.

Skill/Target	YES, I Can!	Skill to work on	NO, I need help.	How important is the skill to me? 1—very, 2—somewhat, 3—not important
1. Plays with puzzles or games				
2. Sorts/groups items together				
3. Matches items that are identical				
4. Recognizs faces/familiar persons				
5. Recognizes home environment				
6.				
7.				
8.				
9.				
10.				

Getting Along

Skill/Target	YES, I Can!	Skill to work on	NO, I need help.	How important is the skill to me? 1–very, 2–somewhat, 3–not important
1. Follows commands to do something (come here, go get something)				
2. Follows a direction to stop				
3. Responds to "no" without behavioral problems				
4. Is willing to participate in self-care activities				
5. Is willing to participate in household chores				
6. Tolerates the removal of items				
7. Tolerates a delay				
8. Tolerates being told to wait				
9. Tolerates transitions				
10. Tolerates loud noises. (examples: music, chatter, children playing, cars, babies crying)				

Self-Care, Hygiene, and Home Participation

Skill/Target	YES, I Can!	Skill to work on	NO, I need help.	How important is the skill to me? 1–very, 2–somewhat, 3–not important
1. Showers and washes hair				
2. Picks out clothes				
3. Gets dressed				
4. Gets undressed				
5. Eats without making a mess				
6. Toilets independently				
7. Cleans up after eating meal				
8. Shaves (face/legs)				
9. Uses and disposes of menstruation products appropriately				
10. Brushes teeth				
11. Brushes hair				
12. Makes bed				
13. Sorts laundry				
14. Washes laundry				
15. Folds laundry				
16. Puts laundry away				
17. Hangs clothes on hangers				
18. Puts dirty clothes in hamper				
19. Showers, washes body				
20. Washes face				
21. Washes hands				
22. Cleans ears				
23. Flosses				
24. Uses mouthwash				
25. Opens containers				
26. Closes containers				

27. Sweeps floors				
28. Vacuums floors				
29. Sets table				
30. Cleans table after eating				
31. Makes a snack				
32. Wipes countertops				
33. Makes bed				
34. Changes sheets on bed				
35. Washes dishes				
36. Loads dishwasher				
37. Unloads dishwasher/puts dishes away				
38. Puts silverware away				
39. Folds towels				
40. Measures detergent for dishwasher				
41. Measures detergent for washing machine				
42. Locks door				
43. Unlocks door				
44. Uses electrical outlets properly				
45. Cleans lint tray in dryer				
46. Gets up with use of alarm clock				
47. Applies deodorant				
48. Applies perfume/ cologne				
49. Clips toenails				
50. Clips fingernails				
51. Participates in dental exam				
52. Participates in physical exam				
53. Knows what to do when fire alarm goes off				

Vocational Skill Ideas

Blank boxes are purposed for parent fill.

Skill/Target	YES, I Can!	Skill to work on	NO, I need help.	How important is the skill to me? 1–very, 2–somewhat, 3–not important
1. Places index cards in envelopes				
2. Assembles toothbrushes in holders				
3. Can package CDs into CD cases				
4. Assembles nut/ washer				
5. Assembles hardware				
6. Counts pencils & puts into cases				
7. Sorts & places together measuring cups				
8. Places keys on key ring				
9. Sorts silverware				
10. Groups brush and mirror & places in ziplock bag				
11. Groups hand towels & clips together				
12. Sorts token chips/tokens & places in tins				
13. Puts items in bags and bins				
14.				
15.				
16.				
17.				
18.				
19.				

Going Public—Environmental Skill Ideas

Blank boxes are purposed for parent fill.

Skill/Target	YES, I Can!	Skill to work on	NO, I need help.	How important is the skill to me? 1–very, 2–somewhat, 3–not important
1. Purchases items from store				
2. Operates vending machine				
3. Creates a food list				
4. Follows a food list				
5. Knows who to ask for help				
6. Can ask for help				
7. Finds a bathroom in a public place				
8. Orders food				
9. Pushes a shopping cart				
10. Follows 2–4 step commands				
11. Uses money				
12. Carries a wallet/purse				
13. Enters new places w/o issue				
14. Exits places w/o issue				
15. Tolerates removal of items				
16. Tolerates denial of items				
17. Can wait appropriately				
18.				

Getting Ready to Be Independent

Skill/Target	YES, I Can!	Skill to work on	NO, I need help.	How important is the skill to me? 1–very, 2–somewhat, 3–not important
1. Unlocks door with keys				
2. Carries keys				
3. Puts on/takes off own seatbelt				
4. Uses a telephone				
5. Picks out own clothing				
6. Ties shoes				
7. Easily uses zippers/buttons on clothing				
8. Uses a debit card correctly				
9. Purchases items using money without assistance				
10. Identifies emergency situations				
11. Identifies changes in weather and what to do				
12. Identifies community helpers/ emergency helpers				
13. Operates entertainment devices (TV, DVD player, etc.)				

Eating/Food Preparation

Skill/Target	YES, I Can!	Skill to work on	NO, I need help.	How important is the skill to me? 1–very, 2–somewhat, 3–not important
1. Operates microwave				
2. Operates stove				
3. Operates toaster				
4. Operates toaster oven				
5. Takes food to table				
6. Uses can opener				
7. Opens/closes Tupperware				
8. Opens/closes ziplock bags				
9. Cleans up after meals				
10. Makes simple snacks				

All Around the Town

Places we go	YES, I enjoy these places!	Places I would like to be included	NO, I prefer not to visit these places.	How important is the skill to me? 1—very, 2—somewhat, 3—not important
1. Parks				
2. Museums				
3. Planetariums				
4. Book store				
5. Music store				
6. Grocery store				
7. Clothing stores/ mall				
8. Food courts/ mall				
9. Trails for walking or biking				
10. Beach				
11. Amusement parks				
12. Markets or fairs				

Enrichment Activities and Leisure Ideas

Activity	YES, I enjoy these activities!	Activities I would like to explore	NO, I do not enjoy these activities.	How important is the skill to me? 1—very, 2—somewhat, 3—not important
1. Books				
2. Movies				
3. Audiobooks				
4. Puzzles				
5. Bike riding				
6. Tetherball				
7. Golf				

8. Wii				
9. Dice				
10. Beads/lacing				
11. Dry erase				
12. Walking				
13. Drawing				
14. Painting				
15. Stencils				
16. Board games				
17. Cross-stitch				
18. Gluing/pasting				
19. Bowling				
20. Hand-held games				
21. Photography				
22. Trampoline				
23. Audio recorders				
24. Swinging				
25. Slides				
26. Climbing				
27. Exploring/finding				
28. Swimming				
29. Walking a dog				
30. Spending time with animals				
31. Ball activities: football, soccer, basketball, tennis, baseball				
32. Rollerblading				

Potential Lessons

Blank boxes are purposed for parent fill.

	YES, I enjoy these activities!	Activities I would like to explore	NO, I do not enjoy these activities.	How important is the skill to me? 1–very, 2–somewhat, 3–not important
1. Tennis				
2. Cooking				
3. Drawing				
4. Music—piano, guitar				
5. Dance				
6. Horseback riding				
7. Swimming				
8. Tumbling				
9. Karate				
10.				

Getting to Work—Job Ideas

Place we go	YES, I enjoy these activities!	Activities I would like to explore	NO, I do not enjoy these activities.	How important is the skill to me? 1—very, 2—somewhat, 3—not important
1. Vet office— helping with the care of pets				
2. Horse stable— helping around stables, feeding, watering				
3. Farm				
4. Grocery store— bagging, stocking, blocking, cleaning				
5. Packaging/line facility				
6. Office/clerical				
7. Plant nursery				
8. Hospital				
9. Housekeeping				
10. Recreation/park				

The Big Stuff—Gross Motor Skills

Skill area	YES, I Can!	Skill to work on	NO, I need help.	How important is the skill to me? 1—very, 2—somewhat, 3—not important
1. Opens car door				
2. Knocks on door				
3. Climbs				
4. Runs				
5. Picks up heavy objects				
6. Plays catch/ball activities				
7. Climbs stairs				
8. Carries items				
9. Loads/unloads items from car or other				
10. Jumps				
11. Walks up and down inclines				

The Little Stuff—Fine Motor Activities

Skill/Target	YES, I Can!	Skill to work on	NO, I need help.	How important is the skill to me? 1—very, 2—somewhat, 3—not important
1. Zippers				
2. Velcro				
3. Buttons				
4. Ties shoes				
5. Snaps				
6. Opens jars, bags, ziplocks				
7. Closes jars, bags, ziplocks				
8. Grasps or holds with entire hand				
9. Grasps or holds with fingers only				
10. Holds writing utensils				
11. Holds eating utensils				
12. Applies pressure with hands when needed				

Chapter 5

Keeping the Good Stuff Going and Stopping the Rest

*Y*ou have come a long way in this workbook. You have identified the behaviors you want to change and those you want to support. You have learned the reasons and motivators behind behaviors, and you should now have a plan in place for how to work on one or more behaviors. Your follow-through, how you consistently practice the new desired behaviors, is the final key to your success.

The environment following a behavior can do one of the following: reinforce the behavior, punish the behavior, or have no effect at all. To reinforce means to increase the likelihood that behavior will occur again; this is keeping the good stuff going. Punishment is meant to cause a decrease in the future likelihood of a behavior occurring. Let's look at some examples of reinforcement.

Reinforcement: Adding or taking away stimuli (environmental elements) that will increase the likelihood that behavior will reoccur

- Asking for juice = juice. Reinforcement: increased asking for juice when wanting it
- Screaming to get a toy = toy given to child. Reinforcement: increased screaming to get toys
- Pushing the power button on remote control = TV turns on. Reinforcement: increased power-button-pushing behavior to get access to the TV
- Working at a job = paycheck. Reinforcement: returning to work for another forty hours

Reinforcement keeps the good stuff going! It is easy to see how reinforcement works. It happens all around us all the time. We may not always be aware of how much reinforcement we come into contact with on a daily basis, but it is always there. Reinforcement has universal elements as well as specific elements. Specific reinforcement is valuable because what is reinforcing to one person may not be reinforcing to another. Your children have specific reinforcers and items they desire or find reinforcing. Reinforcement refers back to the functions of behavior mentioned earlier (remember them?): access, attention, escape, and self-stimulation. Begin to get in tune with what rewards reinforce these four functions in your child. Access to items or activities can be obtained via talking, pointing, screaming, kicking, dropping to the ground, self-injury, or leading. When you are trying to figure out why a behavior occurs or why it does not occur, pay close attention to the environment before the behavior and the environment after the behavior.

The opposite of reinforcement is punishment. Usually people react to the word punishment with negative images of physical consequences or even abuse. This is not what I am referring to. I want you to open your mind and realize that punishment is not hitting your children, spanking them, or causing injury, harm, or fear. Those things do not lead to a change of behavior. Punishment is a consequence following a behavior in which something is added or removed that decreases the likelihood of those behaviors occurring again.

- Throwing toys = loss of TV time. Punishment results: decrease throwing toys
- Cursing = time out. Punishment results: decrease cursing
- Dumping toys out of toy drawers = having to pick up every item two times. Punishment results: decreased dumping toys
- Refusing to eat = loss of dessert. Punishment results: decreased food refusal

Punishment is a consequence that will have an effect on the future frequency of the behavior being punished. It is a consequence. Every person comes into contact with consequences, and your child will not be exempt from consequences in his or her life outside the home. Punishment is ethical, valid, and justified when used properly. It is not OK for your 14-year-old, 175-pound child to throw a tantrum in the middle of the store when told they cannot have a cookie. It is not OK for your adult dependent to throw objects, kick, run away, or engage in self-injurious behavior (SIB) when asked to do something or told to wait or even when he or she hears the word no. It is not acceptable for any person to react and behave in a way that compromises their dignity, endangers themselves or others, or to behave aggressively toward you. Allowing a grown or growing child to behave in ways that are disruptive and harmful is not good for you or them.

The only way to change the behavior is first to understand it:

A. Discover the environment in which it occurs.

B. Learn what the function is.

C. Identify how the environment is reinforcing it.

With the information you have in this workbook, you can develop a strategy in which you are comfortable using appropriate punishment. Punishment might mean you learn to ignore a behavior, remove the reinforcers present when the behavior occurs, implement a time-out procedure, or use restraint. Restraint can be something as simple as touching the person, or it can involve holding down the person's hands, placing the person in her room, which is also a time out, basket holds (this means to sit behind the person and use your body to hold him in a stable position so he can no longer engage in a harmful or destructive behavior), or blocking (this means to prevent the target behavior from occurring). I am not asking you to lay hands on your child in a way that is abusive or threatening or in a manner that triggers fear. I simply ask you to know what you are capable of handling and what can be consistently implemented regardless of the time, place, location, or persons present.

Nothing comes for free. We all behave with the intention of getting something in return. We go to work to get a paycheck. That paycheck represents all the things we can purchase: food, housing, clothing, and entertainment. The same holds true for the children and adults with development delays. They want something in return for their behavior as well. Identifying potential and existing reinforcers will aid you in developing behaviors you would like to continue.

If you need help with identifying reinforcers, refer to Worksheet 5: The Reinforcer Checklist and also participate in Worksheet 6: The Behavior Assessment, both located in the appendix of this book. This is a great way to identify functions of behavior and the events under which certain behaviors take place.

When it comes to reinforcement, remember that reinforcers have a time limit. What works now will not always work later. Have a list of four to five strong reinforcers and several back-up reinforcers ready at your disposal.

Chapter 6

What's Standing in Your Way?

*M*any parents have experienced their share of extreme or difficult problem behaviors in raising their special needs child: hour-long tantrums; destroying of walls, windows, and furniture; food stealing; stripping; elopement; severe aggression toward others; or self-injurious behaviors. These behaviors alone prevent many families from going out in public or developing positive family interactions, and may even cause parents to question their ability to handle their own children.

I encounter families who are at the end of their patience and have begun their search for an assisted living facility for their child. I have seen the anger, stress, and sadness and understand their daily struggle to keep their child functioning in their family. In these cases, I suggest another issue that may be impeding their success in teaching new behaviors: an underlying medical condition. If nothing is working, seek the help of a medical professional who can offer insight to a medical reason that your child may be experiencing and not able to communicate to you.

Many children have underlying medical conditions that are a major contributor to behavioral excesses. These conditions include: headaches, stomachaches, ulcers, toothaches, ticks, anxiety, or a host of other physical or medical conditions. The only way to know that there is something wrong may be that a child is exhibiting aggression, self-injurious behaviors such as head-banging, slapping toward themselves, scratching, or other tissue-damage-causing behaviors. In cases where medical issues are the underlying cause, behavioral interventions cannot decrease or will have limited progress in eliminating those behaviors. Can you imagine if you had an untreated migraine for a month? You would bang your head, too. It can border on unethical to punish behaviors that are caused by a medical issue.

If you have noticed a significant increase in or sudden onset of a behavior that is new or an old reemergent behavior, I would suggest that you first speak with your primary doctor and rule out medical issues.

To rule out extraneous variables, always seek medical attention prior to any medication modification or behavioral interventions. I have encountered many examples of children experiencing pain or other distress due to dental issues or other medical issues such as seizure disorders, medication contraindications, ulcers, earaches, intestinal obstructions, constipation, or near-sightedness, and that distress was the cause of their SIB or aggression.

On a side note, I have experienced many children who have several different doctors who all prescribe medications. I highly suggest you speak with your local pharmacologist where you have your prescriptions filled for their input on the medications you give your child. They are experts in the arena of prescriptions and medications. Do not assume that your doctor knows how all medications interact with other medications.

As your child grows and loses or gains weight, their medications may need to be adjusted to their growing and changing bodies. Medications are a huge factor in the behavior of your child. Another issue to consider in the case of the aging child is puberty.

Just as time won't stay still, puberty will not pass over your child just because he has a developmental disability. It will come and, in some cases, arrive a little earlier. Be prepared; this right of passage can cause discomfort and chaos in his body and your life. Puberty brings an influx of hormones and new frustrations for any child (and their parents!). Many children do not understand the changes going on in their bodies and may experience aggression. Increased needs for food and sleep, crying more often, agitation, restlessness, and general unpleasantness are all part of the season of puberty. Often, parents are not prepared to handle these changes in their child. The most uncomfortable parts of this stage of life are sexual maturity, masturbation, and periods for girls.

Even though many parents are not ready to handle this stage of life, it can be dealt with in a way that is dignified and generally easier to take when you prepare yourself and know what to expect. With girls there are more things to consider. Parents need to have the discussion about what they are going to do about their daughter's periods. There are options to consider such as birth control pills, birth control shots, IUDs, or endometrial ablation. If you decide to allow your daughter to continue menstruation, either naturally or timed with the aid of birth control, training in the use of sanitary products will be necessary. By addressing this topic in a manner that protects your daughter's dignity and self-care, you can rest assured knowing this portion of her care has been handled. Her cleanliness and well-being will become increasingly important as she grows and matures. All these options should be discussed with your doctor or gynecologist who is familiar with your family, as they can advise you of your options in a professional manner.

Should you be the proud parent of a growing boy, you will inevitably find yourself in a position to address his individual effects of puberty as well. I would like to stress that I understand that this can be very uncomfortable to talk about. I haven't experienced a lot of parents who want to talk about this topic openly, but I would really like to emphasize that it is bound to come around and the best way to address it is to be familiar with the possibilities. Should you find yourself at this point, please have a discussion with your family about what you are seeing or experiencing, and maybe it would be a good time to talk with your pediatrician as well. They may be able to direct you in a way that is considerate of your child, your family, and what you feel prepared to handle at that time.

Keep in mind, the prepared parent will be able to handle puberty without all the surprises by planning for them. The parent who hasn't considered all the joys puberty has to offer will be caught off guard and more than likely stressed out by the changes their daughter or son will surely experience. It's not always comfortable, easy, or predictable, but planning ahead will help ease your discomfort with the inevitable.

Seek out the resources in your community as they pertain to you and your family situation.

Part 3

The Path to Peace of Mind

"In three words I can sum up everything I've learned about life: it goes on."

— Robert Frost

Chapter 7

Creating a Plan for the Future

This part of the workbook may be very difficult for you to participate in, or you may not even be able to do it at all yet. But the tragic truth that we must face is that our dependents most likely will outlive us. Having gone through this book, you have worked hard to come up with a behavior plan that gives your child his or her independence. Now you can put that plan on paper and let people know—this is what we want to see for our child when we are gone. Your input and your love and care can extend many years past your physical presence.

When you eventually get to the place in your life when you can no longer care for them, who will? Items such as wills and a designated caregiver are difficult undertakings. By working through those items now, you can save yourself more difficulty in the long run. Before you know it, your dependent will be thirty, then forty, then fifty or sixty. Who will be there to make decisions on his behalf? Who will decide who cares for her? How will those costs be covered?

The following questions will begin the process of walking through how to plan for your child's future. The first steps are to decide or even imagine the age at which your child, teen, or adult dependent will need care that you cannot provide. Whether that age is twenty-two or fifty-two, starting the process now will help with the behavior plan you create for yourself and your child today.

Worksheet 9: Preparing a Plan

Go to www.autismindependence.com to print out a journal log sheet or use a separate sheet of paper to log answers and/or task responses.

Questions to ask:

1. Where do I want my child to live? With family or in a group home?

2. What family members/friends can I count on to help me?

3. What are the group home options?

4. What kind of group home or assisted living facility do I want? Private or paid?

5. What would that cost, approximately?

6. How do I start saving for that now?

7. How will my estate be divided if I pass away?

8. Who will be my child's guardian?

9. What decisions will they have to make?

10. Do I leave specific instructions on how I want my child to live as he or she gets older?

11. Have I planned a will?

12. What steps do I need to take to ensure that my child has the future I wish for him or her?

13. What considerations do I need to make to plan for that future?

All the details you want can and should be planned for, even the details of when they get to go on vacations and trips and who will be their doctor or dentist. You have the privilege of developing an entire life plan with all the details within that plan, including the who, what, when, where, why, and how of the way it is going to be carried out for your child's future.

I suggest you have a meaningful conversation with all parties whom this will affect and discuss your possibilities. They are several agencies that specialize in estate and will planning. This is your opportunity to secure a plan for the future.

Chapter 8

Long-Term Managed Care

If you have reached a point in your journey where the next step is a residential facility, then there are steps you can take to make the transition easier. Prior to this point, I'm assuming you have gone through several emotions that have included guilt, grief, anxiety, and defeat. Maybe you can no longer care for your growing child or address his or her needs. Your child may be too aggressive or too dependent, or you may no longer be able to help your child in a manner that is best for your family. You could be a single parent, retired, aging, or have medical challenges that prevent you from accomplishing the tasks on a day-to-day basis.

Whatever the situation, I am sure you are doing the best you can. I hope you have a support system in place that you can count on to lift you up and reassure you. Regardless, you can still be a part of your child's life and maintain a sense of purpose. I recommend you research the facility which you are considering for placement.

The following checklist will help you in asking some questions when making up your mind.

Worksheet 10: Long-Term Care Planning

Go to www.autismindependence.com to print out a journal log sheet or use a separate sheet of paper to log answers and/or task responses.

1. How close is the residence to my home?
2. How will I communicate with the staff/management regarding my child?
3. How much access will I have to my child?
4. When can I visit?
5. Who will be caring for my child?
6. Is there a nurse on staff?
7. How are behavioral issues addressed?
8. Who oversees staff?
9. What are the qualifications and education of staff and facilitators?

10. What skills are taught in the residence?

11. What are the daily activities and work involved? Is a schedule of events available?

12. Are there any recreational facilities on the property?

13. Are there opportunities for me to bring my child home for weekends and holidays?

If you are considering this option, look for programs that include the following:

1. Cleanliness: facility, grounds, and current residents

2. Well-trained therapists, direct-care providers, and on-staff professionals

3. Background checks of those who come into contact with residents

4. Supervision of direct-care providers

5. TV monitoring or any closed-circuit monitoring system that records video

6. Programs that have meaning in the context of skills being taught

7. Ongoing program monitoring and evaluation

8. Materials and equipment that enrich the participants' lives

9. Activities that are fun, naturalistic, and participatory and that stimulate the residents

10. Encouragement and respect for the active participation of family

11. Open access to your family member(s)

12. Opportunity for choice

Conclusion

You Can Do It!

As your child grows and matures, wonderful opportunities for growth, independence, exploration, and discovery will present themselves. This moment in your life and in the life of your child holds possibility and opportunity. I hope the workbook has opened your eyes to those possibilities and has given you the motivation and desire to take action or to begin the process of being an active participant in the forward motion of your life.

You have all the power and ability to make a difference and every opportunity to make improvements in the outcome of lifelong dignity and independence for your child. Your children are your light and a source of deep love and affection. They are the beauty in your world and deserve independence and dignity in their journey toward adulthood. Good luck and best wishes!

Appendix

Resources, Worksheets, and Printables

1. Daily Schedule Evaluation Worksheet

2. My Child Today Worksheet

3. Skills Inventory Worksheet

4. Skills and Starting Points Worksheet

5. Reinforcer Checklist

6. Behavior Assessment Worksheet

7. Task Analysis for Skills Worksheets

8. Blank Task Analysis for Skills Worksheets

9. Preparing a Plan Worksheet

10. Long-Term Care Planning Worksheet

11. Resources for ABA, Estate Planning, and Managed Care

Go to www.autismindependence.com to print out a journal log sheet or use a separate sheet of paper to log answers and/or task responses.

Worksheet 1: Daily Schedule Evaluation

I. Describe your typical day:

On a separate sheet of paper, describe your day from waking until bedtime. This may help you see the many things you do as a parent.

II. Break it down:

1. Easiest part of your day? Why?

2. Most difficult parts of your day? Why?

3. Part of the day that is the least structured/organized? Is this the easiest part of your day or the most difficult?

4. Part of the day that is most structured/organized? Is this the easiest part of your day or the most difficult?

5. Who are your helpers?

6. If you have help, in what ways do they contribute? How are they most helpful to you?

7. If you do not have help, do you think you need help?

8. If you do need help, where/how can you obtain it?

9. List the things you do for yourself. Examples: manicures, pedicures, exercise, shopping, etc.

10. How much time per day do you allow for yourself?

11. How can you make more time for yourself?

12. How valuable is it to you to have that personal time?

13. Discuss your frustrations. What is breaking you down or preventing you from moving forward?

14. Are there any physical issues that you struggle with?

15. Are there any mental/economic/social/family issues that you struggle with that hinder you from being effective?

16. What are the opportunities you have to participate in your child's therapy?

17. Are there any skills you could be learning alongside your child during therapy?

18. What are the things that get in your way? How do you become immobilized and in which situation(s)?

19. Are you able to release your stress, anxiety, guilt, frustrations? If so, who with?

20. Do you succumb to the pressures of other people's expectations?

21. How can you break those barriers if needed?

Worksheet 2: My Child Today

1. Current age of your child.

2. Your child is affected by _____. Example: autism, Down syndrome, etc.

3. How has this diagnosis affected your child?

4. What are the great things about your child? List all the positive personality characteristics and traits that you admire and adore about your child.

5. What are your child's greatest struggles? List in order of the greatest struggles to the least.

6. What parts of the day are the hardest for your child?

7. What parts of the day are the easiest?

8. Are there any environments in which your child has the most difficulty? Why?

9. Are there any environments in which your child has the easiest time? Why?

10. How many persons interact/are a part of your child's treatment process? (Number of therapists/aides/persons helping with goals)

11. What are your greatest wishes for your child?

12. What do you want your child to accomplish in the next year?

13. What skill(s) do you think your child can/should learn that will make the greatest improvement in her life? (example: toileting, learning to play, etc.)

14. What skills does your child already have that you could help him improve on?

15. Where do you see your child five years from now? Ten years? Fifteen years? Twenty years?

16. Do you have a long-term plan for your child's care when she is an adult?

17. Where can your child work? Or what is your occupational hope for him?

18. Have you assigned/designated a caregiver for your child?

19. How long will you be able to care for your child/meet her day-to-day needs?

20. Do you have a designated caregiver, will, and estate plan should you no longer be able to care for your child?

Worksheet 3: The Skills Inventory

Inventory

What can my child do without any assistance? My child picks up items around the house and places them in an appropriate spot, sorts laundry, gets up in the morning without help.

Is this activity performed repeatedly or occasionally? Every day my child performs these tasks.

How long did it take for my child to learn this skill? She is ten years old and we have been practicing these items pretty much daily for the last couple of years.

How many people can my child do this skill for? He has been able to perform this skill for me consistently and sometimes for others.

Are there any instances where my child will not/refuses to do this activity? She does these things only in our house. I have not sen her perform these actions in other environments.

Roadblocks/obstacles (such as failure to generalize learned skills to other people, places, or environments, special diets, any handicaps, etc.). Sometimes she gets distracted with other activities, such as stimming. She will stop and has to be reminded to finish the task. When other people are in our home, she will not do any of the tasks.

Inventory of Skills and Abilities

Inventory of Skills and Abilities

1. Age of child/teen/adult
2. Likes
3. Interesting activities
4. Barriers/obstacles
5. What can my child do without any assistance?
6. Is this activity performed repeatedly or occasionally?
7. How long will my child attend to a task without interruption?
8. How long did it take for him to learn this skill?
9. How many people can she do this skill for?

10. Are there any instances where he will not/refuses to do this activity?

11. How can this be turned into a functional activity or occupational goal?

12. How many smaller steps can this be broken down into?

13. How many opportunities will she have to practice this skill?

14. How many people will he have to perform this skill for?

15. What kind of special training do I/other participants need?

16. How am I going to do this?

17. Do I need help?

18. If so, who?

19. How much help?

20. What is my time line for this being accomplished?

Worksheet 4: The Skills and Starting Points

Visual Abilities

Skill/Target	YES, I Can!	Skill to work on	NO, I need help.	How important is the skill to me? 1–very, 2–somewhat, 3–not important
1. Plays with puzzles or games				
2. Sorts/groups items together				
3. Matches items that are identical				
4. Recognizs faces/familiar persons				
5. Recognizes home environment				
6.				
7.				
8.				
9.				
10.				

Getting Along

Skill/Target	YES, I Can!	Skill to work on	NO, I need help.	How important is the skill to me? 1–very, 2–somewhat, 3–not important
1. Follows commands to do something (come here, go get something)				
2. Follows a direction to stop				
3. Responds to "no" without behavioral problems				
4. Is willing to participate in self-care activities				
5. Is willing to participate in household chores				
6. Tolerates the removal of items				
7. Tolerates a delay				
8. Tolerates being told to wait				
9. Tolerates transitions				
10. Tolerates loud noises. (examples: music, chatter, children playing, cars, babies crying)				

Self-Care, Hygiene, and Home Participation

Skill/Target	YES, I Can!	Skill to work on	NO, I need help.	How important is the skill to me? 1–very, 2–somewhat, 3–not important
1. Showers and washes hair				
2. Picks out clothes				
3. Gets dressed				
4. Gets undressed				
5. Eats without making a mess				
6. Toilets independently				
7. Cleans up after eating meal				
8. Shaves (face/legs)				
9. Uses and disposes of menstruation products appropriately				
10. Brushes teeth				
11. Brushes hair				
12. Makes bed				
13. Sorts laundry				
14. Washes laundry				
15. Folds laundry				
16. Puts laundry away				
17. Hangs clothes on hangers				
18. Puts dirty clothes in hamper				
19. Showers and washes body				
20. Washes face				
21. Washes hands				
22. Cleans ears				
23. Flosses				
24. Uses mouthwash				
25. Opens containers				
26. Closes containers				

27. Sweeps floors			
28. Vacuums floors			
29. Sets table			
30. Cleans table after eating			
31. Makes a snack			
32. Wipes countertops			
33. Makes bed			
34. Changes sheets on bed			
35. Washes dishes			
36. Loads dishwasher			
37. Unloads dishwasher/puts dishes away			
38. Puts silverware away			
39. Folds towels			
40. Measures detergent for dishwasher			
41. Measures detergent for washing machine			
42. Locks door			
43. Unlocks door			
44. Uses electrical outlets properly			
45. Cleans lint tray in dryer			
46. Gets up with use of alarm clock			
47. Applies deodorant			
48. Applies perfume/ cologne			
49. Clips toenails			
50. Clips fingernails			
51. Participates in dental exam			
52. Participates in physical exam			
53. Knows what to do when fire alarm goes off			

Vocational Skill Ideas

Blank boxes are purposed for parent fill.

Skill/Target	YES, I Can!	Skill to work on	NO, I need help.	How important is the skill to me? 1–very, 2–somewhat, 3–not important
1. Places index cards in envelopes				
2. Assembles toothbrushes in holders				
3. Can package CDs into CD cases				
4. Assembles nut/ washer				
5. Assembles hardware				
6. Counts pencils & puts into cases				
7. Sorts & places together measuring cups				
8. Places keys on key ring				
9. Sorts silverware				
10. Groups brush and mirror & places in ziplock bag				
11. Groups hand towels & clips together				
12. Sorts token chips/ tokens & places in tins				
13. Puts items in bags and bins				
14.				
15.				
16.				
17.				
18.				
19.				

Going Public—Environmental Skill Ideas

Blank boxes are purposed for parent fill.

Skill/Target	YES, I Can!	Skill to work on	NO, I need help.	How important is the skill to me? 1–very, 2–somewhat, 3–not important
1. Purchases items from store				
2. Operates vending machine				
3. Creates a food list				
4. Follows a food list				
5. Knows who to ask for help				
6. Can ask for help				
7. Finds a bathroom in a public place				
8. Orders food				
9. Pushes a shopping cart				
10. Follows 2–4 step commands				
11. Uses money				
12. Carries a wallet/ purse				
13. Enters new places w/o issue				
14. Exits places w/o issue				
15. Tolerates removal of items				
16. Tolerates denial of items				
17. Can wait appropriately				
18.				
19.				

Getting Ready to Be Independent

Skill/Target	YES, I Can!	Skill to work on	NO, I need help.	How important is the skill to me? 1–very, 2–somewhat, 3–not important
1. Unlocks door with keys				
2. Carries keys				
3. Puts on/takes off own seatbelt				
4. Uses a telephone				
5. Picks out own clothing				
6. Ties shoes				
7. Easily uses zippers/buttons on clothing				
8. Uses a debit card correctly				
9. Purchases items using money without assistance				
10. Identifies emergency situations				
11. Identifies changes in weather and what to do				
12. Identifies community helpers/ emergency helpers				
13. Operates entertainment devices (TV, DVD player, etc.)				

Eating/Food Preparation

Skill/Target	YES, I Can!	Skill to work on	NO, I need help.	How important is the skill to me? 1–very, 2–somewhat, 3–not important
1. Operates microwave				
2. Operates stove				
3. Operates toaster				
4. Operates toaster oven				
5. Takes food to table				
6. Uses can opener				
7. Opens/closes Tupperware				
8. Opens/closes ziplock bags				
9. Cleans up after meals				
10. Makes simple snacks				

All Around the Town

Places we go	YES, I enjoy these places!	Places I would like to be included	NO, I prefer not to visit these places.	How important is the skill to me? 1–very, 2–somewhat, 3–not important
1. Parks				
2. Museums				
3. Planetariums				
4. Bookstore				
5. Music store				
6. Grocery store				
7. Clothing stores/ mall				
8. Food courts/mall				
9. Trails for walking or biking				
10. Beach				
11. Amusement parks				
12. Markets or fairs				

Enrichment Activities and Leisure Ideas

Activity	YES, I enjoy these activities!	Activities I would like to explore	NO, I do not enjoy these activities.	How important is the skill to me? 1–very, 2–somewhat, 3–not important
1. Books				
2. Movies				
3. Audiobooks				
4. Puzzles				
5. Bike riding				
6. Tetherball				
7. Golf				
8. Wii				

9. Dice				
10. Beads/lacing				
11. Dry erase				
12. Walking				
13. Drawing				
14. Painting				
15. Stencils				
16. Board games				
17. Cross-stitch				
18. Gluing/pasting				
19. Bowling				
20. Hand-held games				
21. Photography				
22. Trampoline				
23. Audio recorders				
24. Swinging				
25. Slides				
26. Climbing				
27. Exploring/finding				
28. Swimming				
29. Walking a dog				
30. Spending time with animals				
31. Ball activities: football, soccer, basketball, tennis, baseball				
32. Rollerblading				

Potential Lessons

Activity	YES, I enjoy these activities!	Activities I would like to explore	NO, I do not enjoy these activities.	How important is the skill to me? 1–very, 2–somewhat, 3–not important
1. Tennis				
2. Cooking				
3. Drawing				
4. Music—piano, guitar				
5. Dance				
6. Horseback riding				
7. Swimming				
8. Tumbling				
9. Karate				
10.				

Getting to Work—Job Ideas

Place we go	YES, I enjoy these activities!	Activities I would like to explore	NO, I do not enjoy these activities.	How important is the skill to me? 1–very, 2–somewhat, 3–not important
1. Vet office—helping with the care of pets				
2 Horse stable—helping around stables, feeding, watering				
3. Farm				
4. Grocery store—bagging, stocking, blocking, cleaning				
5. Packaging/line facility				
6. Office/clerical				
7. Plant nursery				
8. Hospital				
9. Housekeeping				
10. Recreation/park				

The Big Stuff—Gross Motor Skills

Skill area	YES, I Can!	Skill to work on	NO, I need help.	How important is the skill to me? 1–very, 2–somewhat, 3–not important
1. Opens car door				
2. Knocks on door				
3. Climbs				
4. Runs				
5. Picks up heavy objects				
6. Plays catch/ball activities				
7. Climbs stairs				
8. Carries items				
9. Loads/unloads items from car or other				
10. Jumps				
11. Walks up and down inclines				

The Little Stuff—Fine Motor Activities

Skill/Target	YES, I Can!	Skill to work on	NO, I need help.	How important is the skill to me? 1–very, 2–somewhat, 3–not important
1. Zippers				
2. Velcro				
3. Buttons				
4. Ties shoes				
5. Snaps				
6. Opens jars, bags, ziplocks				
7. Closes jars, bags, ziplocks				
8. Grasps or holds with entire hand				
9. Grasps or holds with fingers only				
10. Holds writing utensils				
11. Holds eating utensils				
12. Applies pressure with hands when needed				

Worksheet 5: The Reinforcer Checklist

Reinforcer	Always preferred item	Sometimes preferred item	Never preferred item	Comes and goes
Television				
TV series or DVDs of those shows				
News/weather/documentary shows				
Game shows				
Disney/cartoon/animated shows				
Movies				
Musical movies				
The credits at the end of movies				
Disney/cartoon/animated movies				
Documentary movies				
Action movies				
Video Games				
Hand-held game devices (Game Boy, DSI)				
Interactives (Wii & Kinetix)				
Controller games (old fashioned/Pac-Man/joystick games)				
Music				
Rock				
Rap				
Pop				
Classical				
Kids' music (children singing)				
Faith-based				
Other				
Sensory & Movement				
Rice or sand play				
Foam/silly string				
Paint				
Bubbles				
Water play				
Jumping				

Reinforcer	Always preferred item	Sometimes preferred item	Never preferred item	Comes and goes
Running				
Spinning				
Bouncing				
Swinging				
Climbing				
Lights: lighted ropes				
Lights: light balls/toys				
Lights: flashlights or spinner lighted toys				
Lights: projector lights (lights on ceilings or walls)				
Being smashed (by pillows)				
Parachutes and blankets				
Bike riding				
Scooters or skateboards				
Roller blades				
Strollers, if applicable				
Car/van/bus/truck rides				
Roller coasters				
Amusement rides				
Tunnels/tents/confined places				
Around the House				
Books – regular				
Books – electronic				
Books – with interactive pieces (flaps, pop-ups, etc.)				
Cars/trucks/trains				
Ramps and tunnels				
Drawing				
Balloons				
Toys with music				
Toys with lights				
Toys with lights and music				
Climbing on counters/ couches/chairs/bed				

Reinforcer	Always preferred item	Sometimes preferred item	Never preferred item	Comes and goes
Dolls/babies/action figures				
Spinning/flicking items (self-stim activities)				
Spinning				
Foods & Beverages				
(Because these items are specific to your child, please list all the items you can think of that they like or have enjoyed.)				
Outdoors & Public Places				
Outdoor parks/playgrounds				
Amusement parks				
Grocery store				
Mall				
Bookstore				
Places of therapy				
Beach				
Movie theater				
Bounce house places				
Indoor playgrounds				
Zoo				
Woods/nature walks				
School				
Relative's house				
Motels/hotels				
Pool				
Church/synagogue/other				
Restaurants/places to eat				

Reinforcer	Always preferred item	Sometimes preferred item	Never preferred item	Comes and goes
What other things can you think of? People, places, things, or activities not found above				

Worksheet 6: The Behavior Assessment

I. Target Behavior Identification:

Briefly describe the problem behavior:

_____

_____

II. Problem Analysis

		Yes	No	Sometimes
1.	Is this behavior more likely to occur in task/when given a demand? If yes, fill out section B.			
2.	Is this behavior more likely to occur in the presence of specific people? If yes, fill out section B.			
3.	Is this behavior more likely to occur during specific parts of the day? If yes, fill out section B.			
4.	Is this behavior more likely to occur at a specific location or place? If yes, fill out section B.			
5.	Is this behavior more likely to occur when attention is removed or given to another person?			
6.	Is this behavior likely to occur when person is alone?			
7.	Is this behavior more likely to occur during transitions? If yes, fill out section B.			
8.	Is this behavior more likely to occur when changes are made to the child's schedule?			
9.	Is this behavior more likely to occur when the child has to wait or when there is a delay?			
10.	Is this behavior more likely to occur if an activity is interrupted? Is yes, fill out section B.			

A. Questions:

1. Is/are there any medication(s) that may affect the child's behavior?

   _____

   _____

2. Is/are there any medical condition(s) that may affect the child's behavior? Example: asthma, allergies, rashes, seizures, etc.

   _____

   _____

3. Does the child have regular sleep patterns? If not, describe the disruptions.

   _____

   _____

4. Does your child have normal eating habits? Example: does he/she refuse to eat? Eat a limited variety of items? Describe any unusual/particular eating habits.

   _____

   _____

5. How many activities does your child engage in? List all therapies, regularly scheduled activities, and times/days per week they take place.

   _____

   _____

6. List number of persons who care for your child and the frequency with which they are with other caregivers.

   _____

   _____

7. Does your child have a home communication system? If so, describe what it is and how often the child uses that communication form.

   _____

   _____

8. If your child has a communication system in place, are there any times, places, or persons at or with which he/she doesn't communicate? Please list.

_____

_____

9. Are there any times of day that the child is allowed to make choices? Have free time? Please detail those times.

_____

_____

B. Events and situations that predict behavior:

1. Time of day: At what time of day are behaviors most and least likely to occur?

   Most likely: _____

   Least likely: _____

2. Settings: In what places are behaviors most and least likely to occur?

   Most likely: _____

   Least likely: _____

3. Person(s): With whom are behaviors most and least likely to occur?

   Most likely: _____

   Least likely: _____

4. Activities: During which activities are behaviors most and least likely to occur?

   Most likely: _____

   Least likely: _____

5. Transitions: During which transitions are behaviors most and least likely to occur?

   Most likely: _____

   Least likely: _____

6. Interruptions: During which interruptions are behaviors most and least likely to occur?

   Most likely: _____

   Least likely: _____

C. Effectiveness of behavior:

1. How much physical effort does the child exhibit during the behavior?

   _____

   _____

2. What is the result of the child engaging in the behavior? Does he/she get what they want? Every time? Occasionally?

   _____

   _____

3. How much time is involved in the behavior?

   _____

   _____

4. How much time elapses before the child gets what he or she wants if he or she receives reinforcement for the behavior?

   _____

   _____

5. Does any particular caregiver give in?

   _____

   _____

6. Are there siblings in the home? How many are there and what are their ages?

   _____

   _____

Worksheet 7: Task Analysis for Skills Worksheets

Task Analysis: Brush Hair

It is assumed the brush is already present and in front of the person.

Score each step as independent or prompted (needed assistance).

6. PLACE BRUSH BACK DOWN										
5. BRUSH FRONT 3X										
4. BRUSH LEFT SIDE 3X										
3. BRUSH RIGHT SIDE 3X										
2. BRUSH BACK OF HAIR 3X										
1. P/U BRUSH										
Training session #	1	2	3	4	5	6	7	8	9	10
Date										

Task Analysis: Brush Teeth

This is a very dense task analysis. If you would like a simplified version, please use a blank sheet and create one that best suits your needs.

Score each step as independent or prompted (needed assistance).

36. WIPE OFF HANDS AND MOUTH W/ TOWEL											
35. SET DOWN CUP											
34. SPIT OUT WATER											
33. SWISH WATER IN MOUTH											
32. SIP SMALL AMOUNT OF WATER											
31. BRING CUP TO MOUTH											
30. FILL CUP WITH WATER											
29. P/U CUP											
28. SET TOOTHBRUSH IN HOLDER											
27. RINSE TOOTHBRUSH											
26. TURN ON WATER											
25. REMOVE TOOTHBRUSH FROM MOUTH											
24. BRUSH TONGUE 3X											
23. TURN BRUSH OVER											
22. BRUSH UPPER RIGHT 3X (flat portion of the tooth)											
21. TURN BRUSH OVER											
20. BRUSH LOWER RIGHT 3X (flat portion of the tooth)											
19. OPEN MOUTH											

18. BRUSH RIGHT SIDE 3X										
17. BRING TOOTHBRUSH TO RIGHT SIDE										
16. BRUSH FRONT TEETH 3X										
15. CLOSE MOUTH										
14. BRING TOOTHBRUSH TO FRONT TEETH										
13. BRUSH UPPER LEFT 3X (flat portion of tooth)										
12. TURN BRUSH OVER										
11. BRUSH LOWER LEFT 3X (flat portion of tooth)										
10. OPEN MOUTH										
9. BRUSH OUTSIDE LEFT 3X										
8. PLACE TOOTHBRUSH ON LEFT SIDE										
7. OPEN MOUTH										
6. BRING TOOTHBRUSH TO MOUTH										
5. SET DOWN TOOTHPASTE										
4. SQUEEZE TOOTHPASTE ON BRUSH										
3. P/U TOOTHBRUSH										
2. OPEN CAP ON TOOTHPASTE										
1. P/U TOOTHPASTE										
Training session #	1	2	3	4	5	6	7	8	9	10
Date										

Task Analysis: Clean Table

Score each step as independent or prompted (needed assistance).

	1	2	3	4	5	6	7	8	9	10
10. RETURN BASKET TO CORRECT DRAWER										
9. P/U BASKET										
8. THROW AWAY PAPER TOWEL										
7. WIPE TABLE 2X WITH PAPER TOWEL										
6. TAKE OUT/P/U PAPER TOWEL										
5. PUT SPRAY BOTTLE BACK IN BASKET										
4. SPRAY BOTTLE 2X										
3. TAKE OUT SPRAY BOTTLE										
2. TAKE BASKET TO TABLE										
1. GET BASKET W/ ALL SUPPLIES FROM DRAWER										
Training session #	1	2	3	4	5	6	7	8	9	10
Date										

Task Analysis: Clothes in Dresser

Score each step as independent or prompted (needed assistance).

11. CONTINUE UNTIL ALL ITEMS ARE PLACED AWAY										
10. CLOSE DRESSER										
9. PLACE ITEM INSIDE										
8. P/U NEXT CLOTHING ITEM										
7. OPEN NEXT DRAWER										
6. CLOSE DRAWER										
5. PLACE CLOTHING ITEM IN DRAWER										
4. P/U ITEM TO BE PUT AWAY										
3. OPEN DRESSER DRAWER										
2. SET BASKET DOWN										
1. TAKE BASKET OF FOLDED CLOTHES TO DRESSER										
Training session #	1	2	3	4	5	6	7	8	9	10
Date										

Task Analysis: Fold Pants/Shorts

Score each step as independent or prompted (needed assistance).

10. PLACE IN LAUNDRY BASKET										
9. SMOOTH OUT PANTS										
8. RELEASE										
7. FOLD OVER TO MEET THE LEFT SIDE										
6. W/ RIGHT HAND P/U RIGHT SIDE OF PANTS										
5. RELEASE CORNERS										
4. BRING LEG AND WAISTBAND UP TO THE OPPOSITE SIDE										
3. P/U PANTS BY LEG AND WAISTBAND (They will be closest to learner because they are horizontal.)										
2. PLACE PANTS FLAT ON TABLE HORIZONTALLY (Pants will be sideways.)										
1. TAKE PANTS OUT OF BASKET										
Training session #	1	2	3	4	5	6	7	8	9	10
Date										

Task Analysis: Fold Socks

Score each step as independent or prompted (needed assistance).

8. PLACE IN LAUNDRY BASKET										
7. SMOOTH FOLDED SOCKS FLAT										
6. FOLD OVER TO THE LEFT										
5. WITH RIGHT HAND GRAB THE BANDS OF BOTH SOCKS										
4. PLACE 2ND SOCK ON TOP OF 1ST SOCK										
3. TAKE 2ND SOCK OUT OF BASKET										
2. PLACE 1st SOCK FLAT ON TABLE										
1. TAKE 1st SOCK FROM BASKET										
Training session #	1	2	3	4	5	6	7	8	9	10
Date										

Task Analysis: Fold Underwear

Score each step as independent or prompted (needed assistance).

10. PLACE IN LAUNDRY BASKET										
9. SMOOTH OUT UNDERWEAR										
8. RELEASE										
7. FOLD UP TO MEET THE TOP										
6. PICK UP BOTTOM OF UNDERWEAR										
5. RELEASE										
4. BRING THE RIGHT SIDE TO THE LEFT SIDE										
3. PICK UP RIGHT SIDE OF UNDERWEAR W/RIGHT HAND										
2. PLACE UNDERWEAR FLAT ON TABLE										
1. TAKE UNDERWEAR OUT OF BASKET										
Training session #	1	2	3	4	5	6	7	8	9	10
Date										

Task Analysis: Get Dressed

Score each step as independent or prompted (needed assistance).

22. PULL SHIRT DOWN OVER BELLY										
21. PLACE LEFT ARM IN LEFT SLEEVE										
20. PLACE RIGHT ARM IN RIGHT SLEEVE										
19. PULL SHIRT OVER HEAD										
18. P/U SHIRT FROM BED										
17. PULL SHORTS UP REMAINDER OF WAY										
16. STAND UP										
15. PULL SHORTS UP AS FAR AS POSSIBLE WHILE SITTING										
14. PLACE LEFT LEG IN LEG HOLE										
13. PLACE RIGHT LEG IN LEG HOLE										
12. BEND FORWARD AT WAIST WITH SHORTS IN HANDS										
11. SIT ON BED										
10. P/U SHORTS										
9. PULL UNDERWEAR UP REMAINDER OF WAY										
8. STAND UP										
7. PULL UNDERWEAR UP AS FAR AS POSSIBLE WHILE SITTING										
6. PLACE LEFT LEG IN LEG HOLE										
5. PLACE RIGHT LEG IN LEG HOLE										
4. BEND FORWARD AT WAIST WITH UNDERWEAR IN HANDS										
3. SIT ON BED										
2. P/U UNDERWEAR										
1. WALK TO BED (WHERE CLOTHES ARE LAID OUT)										
Training session #	1	2	3	4	5	6	7	8	9	10
Date										

Task Analysis: Hang Shirts

Score each step as independent or prompted (needed assistance).

	1	2	3	4	5	6	7	8	9	10
8. PLACE HANGER ON LINE										
7. WALK TO LINE										
6. TAKE HANGER BY THE TOP										
5. PUT LEFT SIDE OF HANGER IN THE SHIRT										
4. PUT RIGHT SIDE OF HANGER IN THE SHIRT										
3. P/U HANGER										
2. LOCATE NECKHOLE										
1. TAKE SHIRT OUT OF BASKET										
Training session #	1	2	3	4	5	6	7	8	9	10
Date										

Task Analysis: Doing the Laundry

Score each step as independent or prompted (needed assistance).

Step										
22. PUSH START										
21. TURN DIAL TO MARKER										
20. CLOSE DRYER DOOR										
19. PLACE DRYER SHEET INTO DRYER										
18. PICK UP DRYER SHEET										
17. PLACE WET CLOTHES INTO DRYER										
16. PULL OUT WET CLOTHES										
15. OPEN LID TO WASHING MACHINE										
14. WHEN WASHER IS FINISHED, OPEN LID TO DRYER										
13. PULL DIAL TOWARD SELF										
12. TURN DIAL TO THE LEFT WHERE MARK IS MADE										
11. PLACE CAP BACK ON DETERGENT										
10. CLOSE LID OF WASHING MACHINE										
9. POUR LIQUID INTO WASHING MACHINE										
8. REMOVE HAND PRESSING ON NOZZLE										
7. FILL CAP WITH DETERGENT TO LINE										
6. WITH OPPOSITE HAND PRESS NOZZLE										
5. PLACE CAP UNDER DETERGENT NOZZLE										
4. TAKE CAP OFF OF DETERGENT										
3. PUT ALL DIRTY CLOTHES INTO THE WASHER										
2. OPEN LID OF WASHING MACHINE										
1. GO TO WASHING MACHINE										
Training session #	1	2	3	4	5	6	7	8	9	10
Date										

Task Analysis: Make a Snack (Peanut Butter w/ Rice Cake)

Score each step as independent or prompted (needed assistance).

14. EAT SNACK										
13. PUT PEANUT BUTTER AWAY										
12. SCREW LID ON TIGHT										
11. PLACE LID BACK ON PEANUT BUTTER JAR										
10. P/U LID										
9. SET DOWN USED KNIFE										
8. SPREAD PEANUT BUTTER ON RICE CAKE										
7. REMOVE SMALL AMOUNT OF PEANUT BUTTER ON KNIFE										
6. PUT KNIFE INTO PEANUT BUTTER JAR										
5. P/U KNIFE										
4. PLACE LID ON TABLE										
3. OPEN LID TO PEANUT BUTTER										
2. PLACE PEANUT BUTTER ON TABLE										
1. P/U JAR OF PEANUT BUTTER										
Training session #	1	2	3	4	5	6	7	8	9	10
Date										

Task Analysis: Put Groceries Away

Score each step as independent or prompted (needed assistance).

	1	2	3	4	5	6	7	8	9	10
9. CONTINUE UNTIL ITEMS ARE PUT AWAY										
8. CLOSE DOOR										
7. PLACE ITEM INSIDE										
6. OPEN CABINET OR REFRIGERATOR										
5. P/U 1 ITEM AT A TIME AND FIND MATCHING PICTURE										
4. PLACE ITEMS ON COUNTER										
3. REMOVE ITEMS FROM BAG										
2. PLACE BAG(S) ON COUNTER										
1. TAKE BAG OF GROCERIES TO COUNTER										
Training session #	1	2	3	4	5	6	7	8	9	10
Date										

Task Analysis: Set the Table

Before the task begins, have the table placemat on the table before learner. Also have the utensils and flatware next to placemat before beginning.

Score each step as independent or prompted (needed assistance).

10. PLACE CUP										
9. P/U CUP										
8. PLACE KNIFE										
7. P/U KNIFE										
6. PLACE SPOON										
5. P/U SPOON										
4. PLACE PLATE										
3. P/U PLATE										
2. PLACE FORK										
1. P/U FORK										
Training session #	1	2	3	4	5	6	7	8	9	10
Date										

Task Analysis: Showering

This one is blank for you to fill in depending on the number of steps your learner uses when showering. This is your opportunity to make the skill as intensive or as easy as possible for your child to learn.

Score each step as independent or prompted (needed assistance).

Training session #	1	2	3	4	5	6	7	8	9	10
Date										

Task Analysis: Sort Dishes

Score each step as independent or prompted (needed assistance).

6. CAN PLACE ANY NUMBER OF DISHES IN ANY ORDER										
5. CAN PLACE 5 OF EACH ITEM (CUP, PLATE, BOWL)										
4. CAN PLACE 4 OF EACH ITEM (CUP, PLATE, BOWL)										
3. CAN PLACE 3 OF EACH ITEM (CUP, PLATE, BOWL)										
2. CAN PLACE 2 OF EACH ITEM (CUP, PLATE, BOWL)										
1. CAN PLACE 1 OF EACH ITEM (CUP, PLATE, BOWL)										
Training session #	1	2	3	4	5	6	7	8	9	10
Date										

Task Analysis: Sort Laundry

The goal is for learner to place 3 items of each color (black & white) into the correct basket 100 percent of the time when the Sd is issued.

Start with three baskets on the floor. In one basket will be all the laundry for sorting. In the second basket place a white clothing item. In the third basket place a black clothing item.

Score each step as independent or prompted (needed assistance).

7. CAN SORT ENTIRE BASKET REGARDLESS OF AMOUNT										
6. CAN SORT 6 PCS OF EACH COLOR										
5. CAN SORT 5 PCS OF EACH COLOR										
4. CAN SORT 4 PCS OF EACH COLOR										
3. CAN SORT 3 PCS OF EACH COLOR										
2. CAN SORT 2 PCS OF EACH COLOR										
1. CAN SORT 1 PC OF EACH COLOR										
Training session #	1	2	3	4	5	6	7	8	9	10
Date										

Task Analysis: Sort Silverware

The goal is for learner to place each of the silverware items into the correct position 100 percent of the time when the Sd is issued.

Start with the silverware tray in front of student with one piece of each item already in its correct position. Issue the Sd.

Score each step as independent or prompted (needed assistance).

6. CAN PLACE ALL PIECES WHEN GIVEN ALL AT ONCE										
5. CAN PLACE 5 OF EACH ITEM (FORK, SPOON, KNIFE)										
4. CAN PLACE 4 OF EACH ITEM (FORK, SPOON, KNIFE)										
3. CAN PLACE 3 OF EACH ITEM (FORK, SPOON, KNIFE)										
2. CAN PLACE 2 OF EACH ITEM (FORK, SPOON, KNIFE)										
1. CAN PLACE 1 OF EACH ITEM (FORK, SPOON, KNIFE)										
Training session #	1	2	3	4	5	6	7	8	9	10
Date										

Task Analysis: Wash Hands

Score each step as independent or prompted (needed assistance).

11. THROW PAPER TOWEL IN THE TRASH										
10. DRY HANDS										
9. GET PAPER TOWEL										
8. TURN WATER OFF										
7. RINSE HANDS										
6. RUB LEFT OVER RIGHT										
5. RUB RIGHT OVER LEFT										
4. RUB HANDS TOGETHER										
3. PUMP SOAP 1X										
2. WET HANDS										
1. TURN WATER ON										
Training session #	1	2	3	4	5	6	7	8	9	10
Date										

Task Analysis: Tie Shoes

Score each step as independent or prompted (needed assistance).

	1	2	3	4	5	6	7	8	9	10
8. PULL TO TIGHTEN LACES										
7. PULL LACE UNDER AND THROUGH										
6. WRAP SHOELACE AROUND LOOP										
5. MAKE LOOP WITH LACE										
4. PULL LACE										
3. TUCK ONE LACE UNDER (USE LEFT OR RIGHT DEPENDING ON DOMINANT HAND)										
2. CROSS THE LACES										
1. PICK UP BOTH SHOELACES										
Training session #	1	2	3	4	5	6	7	8	9	10
Date										

Task Analysis: Wash Hair

Score each step as independent or prompted (needed assistance).

12. RINSE HAIR										
11. RUB SHAMPOO INTO HAIR FOR PRESELECTED AMOUNT OF TIME OR NUMBER OF TIMES										
10. PLACE SHAMPOO WITH BOTH HANDS INTO HAIR										
9. RUB HANDS TOGETHER TO DISTRIBUTE SHAMPOO TO BOTH HANDS										
8. RETURN BOTTLE TO RESTING PLACE IF NOT USING PUMP BOTTLE										
7. REPLACE LID IF NECESSARY										
6. COLLECT SHAMPOO IN OPEN HAND										
5. SQUEEZE SHAMPOO BOTTLE IF NECESSARY										
4. TURN BOTTLE UPSIDE DOWN										
3. OPEN SHAMPOO BOTTLE / PUMP IF CONTAINER HAS A PUMP										
2. P/U SHAMPOO BOTTLE										
1. WET HAIR										
Training session #	1	2	3	4	5	6	7	8	9	10
Date										

Task Analysis: Clean Up After Meals

Fill in with the number of items your learner incorporates into their mealtime routine.

Score each step as independent or prompted (needed assistance).

Training session #	1	2	3	4	5	6	7	8	9	10
Date										

Task Analysis: Make the Bed

This one is blank for you to fill in depending on the number of bed coverings your learner uses. This is your opportunity to make the skill as intensive or as easy as possible for your child to learn.

Score each step as independent or prompted (needed assistance).

Training session #	1	2	3	4	5	6	7	8	9	10
Date										

Task Analysis: Putting on Deodorant

Score each step as independent or prompted (needed assistance).

15. REPLACE CAP BACK ONTO DEODORANT										
14. LOWER ARM										
13. PLACE DEODORANT DOWN										
12. RUB DEODORANT STICK UP & DOWN FOR PREDETERMINED NUMBER OF TIMES										
11. RAISE DEODORANT INTO POSITION										
10. LIFT UP REMAINING ARM										
9. SWITCH HANDS										
8. LOWER ARM										
7. PLACE DEODORANT DOWN										
6. RUB DEODORANT STICK UP & DOWN FOR PREDETERMINED NUMBER OF TIMES										
5. RAISE DEODORANT INTO POSITION										
4. LIFT UP FIRST ARM FOR APPLICATION										
3. PLACE LID ON COUNTER										
2. REMOVE LID WITH FREE HAND										
1. WITH DEODORANT IN FRONT OF LEARNER, HAVE THEM HOLD THE DEODORANT IN ONE HAND										
Training session #	1	2	3	4	5	6	7	8	9	10
Date										

Worksheet 8: Blank Task Analysis for Skills Workshheets

Task Analysis: Blank

Score each step as independent or prompted (needed assistance).

	1	2	3	4	5	6	7	8	9	10
Training session #	1	2	3	4	5	6	7	8	9	10
Date										

Task Analysis: Blank

Score each step as independent or prompted (needed assistance).

	1	2	3	4	5	6	7	8	9	10
Training session #	1	2	3	4	5	6	7	8	9	10
Date										

Task Analysis: Blank

Score each step as independent or prompted (needed assistance).

Training session #	1	2	3	4	5	6	7	8	9	10	
Date											

Task Analysis: Blank

Score each step as independent or prompted (needed assistance).

Training session #	1	2	3	4	5	6	7	8	9	10
Date										

Task Analysis: Blank

Score each step as independent or prompted (needed assistance).

	1	2	3	4	5	6	7	8	9	10
Training session #	1	2	3	4	5	6	7	8	9	10
Date										

Task Analysis: Blank

Score each step as independent or prompted (needed assistance).

Training session #	1	2	3	4	5	6	7	8	9	10
Date										

Worksheet 9: Preparing a Plan

Questions to ask:

1. Where do I want my child to live? With family or in a group home?

2. Which family members/friends can I count on to help me?

3. What are the group home options?

4. What kind of group home or assisted living facility do I want? Private or paid?

5. What would that cost, approximately?

6. How do I start saving for that now?

7. How will my estate be divided if I pass away?

8. Who will be my child's guardian?

9. What decisions will they have to make?

10. Do I leave specific instructions on how I want my child to live as he or she gets older?

11. Have I planned a will?

12. What steps do I need to take to ensure that my child has the future I wish for him or her?

13. What considerations do I need to make to plan for that future?

Worksheet 10: Long-Term Care Planning

1. How close is the residence to my home?

2. How will I communicate with the staff/management regarding my child?

3. How much access will I have to my child?

4. When can I visit?

5. Who will be caring for my child?

6. Is there a nurse on staff?

7. How are behavioral issues addressed?

8. Who oversees staff?

9. What are the qualifications and education of staff and facilitators?

10. What skills are taught in the residence?

11. What are the daily activities and work involved? Is a schedule of events available?

12. Are there any recreational facilities on the property?

13. Are there opportunities for me to bring my child home for weekends and holidays?

If you are considering this option, look for programs that include the following:

1. Cleanliness: facility, grounds, and current residents

2. Well-trained therapists, direct-care providers, and on-staff professionals

3. Background checks of those who come into contact with residents

4. Supervision of direct-care providers

5. TV monitoring or any closed-circuit monitoring system that records video

6. Programs that have meaning in the context of skills being taught

7. Ongoing program monitoring and evaluation

8. Materials and equipment that enrich the participants' lives

9. Activities that are fun, naturalistic, and participatory and that stimulate the residents

10. Encouragement and respect for the active participation of family

11. Open access to your family member(s)

Worksheet 11: Resources for ABA, Estate Planning, and Managed Care

I. Applied Behavior Analysis/Verbal Behavior Resources:

www.appliedbehaviorcenter.com

www.bacb.com

www.abainternational.org

fabaworld.org

www.establishingoperationsinc.com

rsaffran.tripod.com/aba.html

II. Residential Living Resources:

www.new-horizons.org/hougrh.html

trainland.tripod.com/residential.htm

Florida: Agency for Persons with Disabilities

www.abletrust.org/links/agency_listings_CF.shtml

III. Estate Planning and Will Preparation

www.autismtoday.com/articles/Special_Needs_Trusts_Estate_Planning.htm

www.nami.org/Content/NavigationMenu/Find_Support/Legal_Support/Special_Needs_Estate_Planning_Resources.htm

www.familyvillage.wisc.edu/general/estate.htm

www.womenetics.com/finance/1693-estate-planning-tips-for-families-with-special-needs

IV. Autism Information

www.autismspeaks.org

www.autism-society.org

www.cureautismnow.org

You can also find more information and links on my website at www.autismindependence.com.

If you're a fan of this book, please tell others...

- Write about *Autism, Adolescence, and Adulthood* on your blog, Twitter, MySpace, and Facebook page.

- Suggest *Autism, Adolescence, and Adulthood* to friends.

- When you're in a bookstore, ask them if they carry the book. The book is available through all major distributors, so any bookstore that does not have *Autism, Adolescence, and Adulthood* in stock can easily order it.

- Write a positive review of *Autism, Adolescence, and Adulthood* on www.amazon.com.

- Send my publisher, HigherLife Publishing, suggestions on Web sites, conferences, and events you know of where this book could be offered at media@ahigherlife.com.

- Purchase additional copies to give away as gifts.

Connect with me...

To learn more about *Autism, Adolescence, and Adulthood*, please contact me at bbarber@autismindependence.com, visit my website at www.autismindependence.com, or you can friend me on facebook at autismindependence.

You may also contact my publisher directly:
HigherLife Publishing
400 Fontana Circle
Building 1 – Suite 105
Oviedo, Florida 32765
Phone: (407) 563-4806
Email: media@ahigherlife.com